Praise for *Your IEP Playbook*

"Lisa Lightner is a force in the world of special education advocacy. As the founder of A Day in Our Shoes, Lisa has created a lifeline for countless families who often feel isolated, overwhelmed, and underinformed in the IEP process. This book is the natural extension of more than a decade of tireless, hands-on work supporting parents—grounded in deep expertise, unwavering empathy, and real-life results."
—**Laura Sullivan Heneghan,** Special Education Attorney

"Lisa Lightner delivers advocacy advice in a parent friendly format that will leave you with a well-prepared seat at the IEP table."
—**Mandy Colville,** advocate

"*Your IEP Playbook* is an essential guide for any parent navigating every step of the IEP process. As an occupational therapist, I appreciate how this book breaks down the entire IEP process into clear, manageable steps. The unique sports-themed 'playbook' format is both engaging and practical, giving parents actionable 'plays' to implement at each stage."
—**Colleen Beck,** OTR/L, school-based occupational therapist and owner of The OT Toolbox

"As the parent of a child with disabilities and someone who has done advocacy for 15+ years, I've seen firsthand the need for well-informed advocacy. Lisa Lightner's *Your IEP Playbook* is an incredible guide for parents and families both new to the special education world and those who are seasoned—you can always learn more."
—**Blake Emmanuel,** MPA, Director of Advocacy and Policy for The Fund for Women and Girls and parent of a child with multiple disabilities

Your IEP Playbook

Your IEP Playbook

A Parent's Guide to Confident Advocacy

LISA LIGHTNER

JB JOSSEY-BASS™

A Wiley Brand

Published by John Wiley & Sons, Inc., Hoboken, New Jersey.
Published simultaneously in Canada.
ISBNs: 9781394294466 (paperback), 9781394294503 (ePDF), 9781394294480 (ePub)

For general information on our other products and services or for technical support, please contact our Customer Care Department within the United States at (800) 762-2974, outside the United States at (317) 572-3993 or fax (317) 572-4002.

Wiley also publishes its books in a variety of electronic formats. Some content that appears in print may not be available in electronic formats. For more information about Wiley products, visit our website at **www.wiley.com**.

Library of Congress Control Number: 2025025575 (print)

Cover Design: Wiley
Cover Image: © Eva Kali/stock.adobe.com
Author Photo: Courtesy of the author

For the parents who never stop fighting, the staff who go the extra mile, and the kids at the center of it all—you are the reason this book exists.
May your voices be heard, your efforts be seen, and your paths forward be a little clearer.

Contents

Visit https://adayinourshoes.com/playbook to access the templates in this book.

APPENDIXES Practice Drills 173

Foreword

I do not recall precisely when I first met Lisa Lightner. I do know, however, that when we met, we were on different "teams." I was working as a school district administrator and Lisa was working as a special education advocate for the ARC of Pennsylvania. Far too often, school administrators and advocates take adversarial stances. Too many times, either side can become too focused on "winning" and the needs of the child are sometimes sidelined. What I recognized in Lisa from the start is that her focus is always on the child and what that child needs to learn and to thrive. Her focus has meant that she will challenge the educators but also, at times, parents, when either or both "teams" have lost sight of what is in the best interest of the child. During what too often becomes a battle, Lisa has always understood the need to put the child at the center. I like to believe that I, too, have been someone who strived to always keep the needs of the child in focus. I think that shared focus is what is at the heart of our mutual respect and admiration. Lisa and I are in different roles but we both continue to educate and advocate on behalf of students with disabilities.

Lisa's book takes the reader through the IEP process from start to finish. She begins by placing the laws and rights that students with disabilities currently have in context and explains just how we got to where we are today. That understanding is important not only because it underscores just how recently these rights were established but also because it tells a story of just how powerful parents can be as advocates for their children. Chapter by chapter, Lisa takes the reader through all the steps in the lengthy and often confusing process public schools are required to complete to comply with the mandates of the IDEA. She doesn't simply regurgitate what's in the law; rather she explains and simplifies things in a conversational manner and in language that can be comprehended by parents who don't have degrees in education or years of practice working through the system.

Parents are the target audience for this book but as an experienced educator and advocate, I know that Lisa's knowledge and perspective is useful and important to teachers, psychologists, and other professionals.

In my work teaching graduate students and developing educational content for them, I frequently refer to the online resources she has developed. Once during a class discussion about the important role of parents as part of the multidisciplinary and IEP teams, I cited a post by Lisa while urging the students to refrain from referring to parents as "mom" or "dad" and from calling parents by their first name until invited to do so. At least a half dozen students in the class mentioned seeing that same post and noted how often they refer to Lisa's webpage. I have no doubt that I and many other professionals will be both using and recommending *Your IEP Playbook*.

Dr. Monica McHale-Small,
Director of Education,
Learning Disabilities Association of America

Preface

"Though nobody can go back and make a new beginning... . Anyone can start over and make a new ending."

—Chico Xavier

I hope, if you bought this book, that you're here because you have a child with an individualized education program (IEP). If not, the information in these pages won't be of much use to you just yet. But don't worry; if you're still in the process of trying to get an IEP for your child, Chapter 5 is specifically for you. The same applies if your child currently has a 504 Plan and you think they may need an IEP. Start there.

Once you've tackled that part, come back to the beginning of this book and dive in. This guide is meant to walk you through the IEP process section by section, breaking down each part, explaining the terms, and helping you feel confident navigating the system.

A Quick Note for Urgent Situations

Before we dive in, I want to address a specific group of parents. If your child's situation is urgent—if they're being suspended repeatedly, facing police involvement, or dealing with significant mental health issues like self-harm—please seek professional help immediately.

I hear this all the time: "I can't afford that." But I'm here to tell you, you can't afford *not* to seek help in these situations.

I've never seen an urgent situation like this resolve itself. Whether it's consulting with a special education attorney or working with a private psychologist or psychiatrist, it's worth exploring your options. Many parents are surprised to find that an initial consultation is more affordable than they expected.

If this applies to you, handle the immediate crisis first. Then come back to this book when things have stabilized.

What This Book Covers

The information here applies to every IEP regardless of your child's specific disability. While the interventions or strategies you pursue may vary, the IEP process itself is universal. Whether your child has dyslexia, autism, ADHD, or another disability, this book will give you the tools you need to advocate effectively.

Since 2011, when I started my website (**adayinourshoes.com**), I've had the privilege of working with and advising thousands of parents. I've heard their frustrations, celebrated their victories, and learned from their experiences. I'd love to say, "I've seen it all," but every time I think that, something new surprises me.

Why I Wrote This Book

I started working as a special education advocate in 2010. Since then, I've attended hundreds of IEP meetings, dozens of manifestation determination meetings, and several mediations. I've seen it all: the good, the bad, and the downright absurd.

But here's the thing: This book isn't about me. It's about *you*.

My goals are simple:

- Reduce your stress. The IEP process can feel overwhelming, but it doesn't have to be.
- Increase your confidence. With the right knowledge and tools, you can become a strong advocate for your child.

Even if things are going relatively well right now, the strategies and insights in this book can help you be proactive. Addressing potential issues before they arise is always better than scrambling to fix problems later.

A Reality Check About the IEP Process

Let's get one thing out of the way: The IEP process is slow.

It's not designed to move quickly, and that's often a source of frustration for parents. If you're working through this book and implementing the steps I recommend, be prepared for the process to take weeks or even months.

Again, if your child is in immediate danger—whether from bullying, a mental health crisis, or any other urgent situation—don't wait. Seek help immediately. This might mean calling the police if your child is being physically harmed at school, consulting a crisis counselor, or contacting an attorney. Some situations can't wait, and I'd never want a child's condition to worsen while you work through this book.

Advocates and Schools: A Delicate Balance

The history between advocates and schools is, to put it mildly, contentious.

There's no shortage of IEP teams that bristle at the mention of an advocate attending a meeting. For some, it feels like an adversarial move even if your intent is simply to ensure your child's needs are met. There's no shortage of IEP teams that become visibly uncomfortable—or even defensive—when a parent brings an advocate to a meeting. Sometimes, it's subtle like a change in tone or body language. Other times, it's more direct: They may question your decision, try to limit your advocate's role, or treat it as a sign that you're gearing up for a fight.

But here's the truth: Bringing an advocate doesn't automatically mean things are adversarial. It's not a declaration of war. For most parents, it's a way to level the playing field and ensure that their child's needs are being understood and addressed fully. IEP meetings are emotional, complex, and often overwhelming, especially when you're navigating unfamiliar laws, processes, and acronyms. An advocate can help translate the jargon, ask the right questions, and keep the conversation focused on your child.

Yes, some teams may perceive it as a threat. But your goal isn't to make enemies; instead, it's to make progress. And sometimes, having a knowledgeable support person at the table is what helps shift the dynamic, create accountability, and make sure your voice is truly heard.

Moving Forward Together

This book is designed to be your guide. We'll walk through every section of the IEP, breaking it down into manageable pieces. I'll explain what the law says, what best practices look like, and how to advocate for your child's unique needs. Along the way, I'll share strategies, templates, and real-life examples to help you feel more confident in the process.

Your role as an advocate is crucial. Schools are often stretched thin, and while most educators genuinely care about their students, systemic issues can prevent them from providing what your child needs. That's where you come in. By understanding the IEP process and using your rights effectively, you can ensure your child gets the education they deserve.

Let me be clear: My goal is collaboration.

This book isn't about "getting" the school or punishing teachers. Sure, there are advocates who come in with a nuclear approach from the outset, but that's not my style. I'll attend your IEP meeting, but then I leave. You, on the other hand, have to live and work in that community. You might have other children in the school district. You'll need to maintain those relationships long after I'm gone.

And here's a little nugget from my site analytics: About 20% of parents I work with are teachers themselves or work for the school district. That's an important perspective to keep in mind.

The Truth About Schools

Most teachers are good people. Most IEP teams genuinely believe they're meeting your child's needs. The problem isn't usually a lack of effort; it's a lack of resources.

Even in the wealthiest school districts, resources are finite. That's why IEP issues often boil down to money, not malice. This doesn't mean you should settle for less than what your child needs, but it's important to understand the dynamics at play.

My Advocacy Philosophy

I advocate for your child. Not for you but for your child.

That distinction is critical because advocating for a child sometimes means pushing parents out of their comfort zones. Advocacy requires learning, growing, and, at times, being assertive in uncomfortable situations.

My second goal is to help repair (or preserve) the relationship between you and your school district. This can be challenging, especially if things have gotten contentious. But it's essential. You and the school are in this for the long haul, and a fractured relationship doesn't benefit anyone, least of all your child.

Those goals are the foundation of my advocacy strategy and philosophy, and will carry through to this book. The strategies and insights in this book are designed to empower you, reduce your stress, and help you navigate the IEP process with confidence.

Before we dive in, I want you to remember two things:

1. The IEP process is a marathon, not a sprint.
2. You're not alone.

So, take a deep breath, pour yourself a cup of coffee, and let's get started. We've got this.

Introduction

"Well behaved women seldom make history."

—Laurel Thatcher Ulrich

In the 1950s, a mother named Gladys brought her eight-year-old son Billy* to their neighborhood elementary school in a small Pennsylvania town. At the time, state law required children to be enrolled in school by age eight, and since Gladys had not yet enrolled Billy, she faced the possibility of fines or even arrest.

But Gladys wasn't neglectful or unaware. Billy was intellectually disabled, and she knew—just from living in that community—that the local school had nothing to offer him. There were no special education classrooms, no individualized support, no expectation that children like Billy could learn. In the 1950s, it was assumed that intellectually disabled people were "uneducable" which is a damaging stigma that still exists today. Still, she did what she could: She walked into the principal's office and said, "I want you to meet my son Billy. He's eight years old, but I'm not enrolling him. You don't have anything for him here, and I don't want to get arrested for not sending him."

The principal didn't argue. He didn't try to convince her otherwise. He simply replied, "You're right. We don't have anything for him here. But don't worry, I won't report you."

And that was it. Gladys took Billy home, and he never received a public education. At the time, schools weren't legally required to serve disabled students, and children like Billy were often labeled "uneducable" by doctors and teachers. There was no IDEA, no FAPE, no system of support. Just doors quietly—and permanently—closed.

The Individuals with Disabilities Education Act (IDEA) wouldn't become law for another 20 years. By that time, Billy was an adult.

This anecdote is a true story. I heard Gladys share it in person at a fundraising dinner. She has since passed away, but her story has stayed with me. Gladys spent her entire life fighting for children like Billy, and her courage in the face of institutional failure inspires me to this day.

I've been a professional Special Education Advocate since 2010, and while I often say that my disabled son is my inspiration, it's moms like Gladys who keep me going. In most households, the burden of all the "IEP stuff" falls on moms instead of dads. Most special education advocates are women. I sometimes get pushback for pointing this out, but it's not a criticism of anyone. It's just what "is." By and large, all of this is done by women. The PARC decree came about because of women/moms and that is what set the foundation for IDEA and special education as we know it today.

If Gladys could stand up to a system that outright refused to educate her child, despite having no legal protections or allies, then surely I can do something.

So, welcome to my "something." This book is one way of contributing to the fight for children like Billy, my son, and your child.

In 1972, Pennsylvania finally implemented a special education law, just three years before IDEA was signed into law by President Gerald Ford in 1975. These laws didn't come about because lawmakers suddenly had a change of heart. They came about because parents like Gladys refused to stay silent. They believed in their children's potential and demanded that the world see it too.

Progress and Persistent Challenges

As this book goes to print, we are celebrating the 50th anniversary of IDEA. In many ways, we've come a long way. Public schools can no longer legally deny children with disabilities the right to an education. We have legal frameworks that outline parents' rights, the services schools must provide, and the standards they must meet.

But for those of us in the trenches, who live and breathe the realities of the IEP process, it's clear we still have so far to go.

Kids are still being denied the support and services they need. Schools delay evaluations or provide inadequate ones. Goals are written so vaguely that progress is nearly impossible to measure. And in some of the most heart-wrenching cases, children with disabilities are punished, suspended, arrested, restrained, or secluded, all for behaviors that are manifestations of their disabilities.

The school-to-prison pipeline is a horrifying reality. Kids with learning disabilities, ADHD, autism, or mental health challenges are disproportionately funneled into this pipeline. These are the children who are misunderstood, underserved, and unfairly disciplined, often with life-altering consequences. Fewer than 20% of autistic adults have meaningful employment.

Why Advocacy Matters

Despite 50 years of IDEA, schools are still not set up for success. Funding is inadequate, and while all students feel the effects, disabled students bear the brunt of it. Yet we have the knowledge and tools to do better. We know what curricula work for struggling readers. We know what de-escalation techniques are effective for anxious or autistic students. The data exist. The strategies are out there.

The problem isn't a lack of solutions; it's a lack of implementation.

This is where advocacy comes in. As Maya Angelous said, "Once you know better, you do better."

Most parents don't understand the IEP process, and that's not all their fault. The system is intentionally complex and cumbersome. Add in the emotional weight of advocating for your child while facing resistance, and it's no wonder so many parents feel overwhelmed.

But this lack of understanding can cost your child valuable time and interventions. That's why I'm here: to help you understand the system so you can navigate it effectively.

A Personal Mantra

When my son was an infant, we received his diagnosis after noticing he wasn't meeting developmental milestones. Those early days of specialist visits and genetic testing were a blur. Social media wasn't what it is today: There were no Facebook groups or Instagram accounts dedicated to IEP tips. Parents like me weren't sharing stories or strategies on Myspace.

But YouTube was gaining traction, and someone sent me a link to Randy Pausch's "Last Lecture." If you've never seen it, I highly recommend watching it. Randy was a professor at Carnegie Mellon who, after being diagnosed with terminal cancer, gave a speech that's become legendary.

One line from that lecture has stuck with me ever since: "I cannot change the cards I've been dealt, but I can choose how I play the hand."

Those words became my mantra. My son's diagnosis felt like a devastating hand, but I realized that I had the power to decide how to play it. That's why I call this book a playbook because I want to help you figure out how to play the hand you've been dealt.

You'll also find many sports references and analogies, hence the playbook reference. While IEPs are a huge part of both my personal and professional life, so are sports. My youngest son plays basketball, and we watch a lot of baseball and football in our house. As of 2024, I can add "Fantasy Football Champion" to my resume. Also, go Birds!

The IEP as a Tool for Change

An IEP is more than just a legal document. It's a road map for your child's education and, by extension, their future. But like any road map, it's only useful if it's accurate and well-designed.

Too many children are still being left behind because their IEPs are vague, incomplete, or ignored altogether. Even though we no longer live in a world where children like Billy are turned away at the schoolhouse door, the reality is that many disabled kids are still being denied meaningful access to education.

Here's the good news: You have more power than you realize. You don't need to be a lawyer or an educator to be an effective advocate. What you need is knowledge, persistence, and the willingness to assert your rights.

We've made progress, but there's still so much work to do. Kids like Billy deserve better. Your child deserves better. And, together, we can make that happen.

If you bought this book (thank you, by the way!), you have a disabled child. Those are the cards that we all were dealt. This is the team we've been drafted to. Do you ever watch the NBA or NFL draft, or know how it works?

In both leagues, in an effort to provide fairness and balance, the worst performing teams get to draft players first. So, the best college players, the ones at the top of their game, go to the worst teams.

No, I'm not saying that our kids are the worst. Most IEP parents would agree that the IEP process and meetings are the worst. Not only are we on a team we didn't ask to be on, we have to play all the positions, sometimes simultaneously. We play offense, we play defense, we play special teams.

Not only do we have to play all the positions, but we also are kind of playing on two teams. Because not only do we have to learn the IEP process and advocate for our kids, but we also have to become experts in our kids' specific condition(s). Learning the IEP process puts us on a learning curve. And parenting a child with any type of disability—mild to significant—also puts us on a learning curve. No wonder we feel overwhelmed at times!

We wouldn't do this if we didn't have to. Ok, right, I do this for a living, so I've just contradicted myself and proven my point all at once.

Because my point is this: I was drafted unwillingly. My son was born with a condition that parents neither cause nor prevent. But I took the cards I was dealt and played the hell out of them; not only did what I could to get my child's needs met but put systems in place to help millions of other kids get their needs met.

Not all terrible teams stay terrible. The Patriots were terrible when they drafted Tom Brady. So, you, too, might have a long, successful IEP journey. Just like terrible sports teams work to turn around their win record, we can turn our terrible IEP experiences into something actually enjoyable. Yes, I said you can learn to enjoy IEP meetings.

Just like the top college players don't want to go to a bad team, they acknowledge that's just how it works and they make the best of it. None of us wanted to be drafted to this team, but we're here and there's no going back. Advocacy is a journey, but you don't have to walk it alone.

Your Play for This Chapter

Take a moment to reflect on your own "hand." What cards have you been dealt, and how can you play them to your child's advantage?

PART 1

Welcome to the Draft

We've come a long way. From the days when kids with disabilities were denied a public education altogether, to the passage of landmark laws like IDEA, to the ever-evolving guidance and court rulings that shape what special education looks like today. Understanding how we got here matters because the system we're navigating now wasn't built overnight.

But let's be real: Just knowing the history doesn't automatically make any of this easier. It's one thing to know your rights in theory. It's another thing entirely to walk into an IEP meeting and advocate for your child when the stakes are high and emotions are even higher. It's important, and possibly motivating, to understand where we came from as a segment of society, and the many parents and advocates who fought very hard for what we have.

You didn't ask to be here, but here you are and on the roster. Becoming an IEP parent isn't something anyone trains for, and yet the moment your child is identified for special education, you're in the game. This part of the journey is like draft day: overwhelming, full of unknowns, and yet full of potential.

You might not feel ready, and that's okay. No one walks into the IEP process with all the plays memorized. But this is where your role begins: not just as a parent, but as an advocate, a strategist, and your child's most reliable teammate.

PART I

Welcome to the Diet

CHAPTER 1

Getting Started in Advocacy

"The IEP process never gets easier. You get better."

— Me

Go back and read that quote again. Because it's true. Since 1975, Individuals with Disabilities Education Act (IDEA) has undergone a few revisions and updates and only created more things to know. Not less! One of the most important aspects of advocacy in the individualized education program (IEP) process is both understanding your role and rights as a parent and understanding the IEP process.

To be an effective advocate, loving your children and wanting them to succeed is not enough. In fact, during IEP meetings, it's essential for you to put aside your passion for your child and focus on the business meeting you're about to attend. But more on that in a later chapter.

As far as the IEP process goes, parents don't have a choice of whether or not to advocate for their child. It's not optional. If you do not take ownership of your child's IEP, their progress, and your own rights and advocacy knowledge and advocacy journey, your child will likely get left behind.

Advocacy Can Feel Like a Full-Time Job

Sometimes, depending on the words I choose (and I'm trying to be very intentional here) to tell parents this information or admonishment, it offends parents. I've been told that it's too harsh, abrasive, uncaring, or unsympathetic to the challenges that parents face. Nothing could be further from the truth. My family has lots of challenges, too, and I'm not suggesting that any parent advocate every day, five days a week.

When your child gets a diagnosis, there will be a lot of sad feelings. The IEP process is overwhelming, confusing, aggravating, and more. That's exactly why I do what I do: I explain these things in a way that parents can understand and use the information.

But no matter what your challenges are, at some point, we have to get up, dust ourselves off, and say, "Ok, I am going to take one step at a time and do this." Because again, if you do not advocate for your child, no one will. No one cares about your IEP more than you do.

IDEA and the state regulations for special education have many defined procedures to follow. Things that might seem like common sense in the IEP process often are anything but. Parents must step out of their comfort zone and commit to learning this. I get it. We're all busy. We work, we have other kids, we'd like to have some time for ourselves. Learning all about IEPs certainly wasn't on my radar when I had Kevin all those years ago.

Learning the IEP process will help you be a better and more effective advocate for your child. It will actually be less stressful for you because I've found that a big piece of parents' stress in this process is the uncertainty.

Reading the Statutes

If you know the IEP process, it's less likely that you'll be taken advantage of. Again, this is not a school-bashing book. But some IEP teams take advantage of what parents don't know. A school staff person can word things to you in a way that isn't incorrect or against IDEA, but doesn't tell the full story either.

There's no getting around it. You have to learn this if you want to change your child's outcomes. I will provide you with practical knowledge, but there are no shortcuts. So often I hear from parents who reach out to me to be their advocate, and they say things like, "But I do speak up at meetings. I do advocate for him."

Showing up at a meeting once a year and voicing your opinion on your child's IEP is not enough. You must use the outlined process by IDEA so the child sitting at your kitchen table matches the child described on the IEP. And just asking for that is not enough. IDEA is a federal statute. I don't know how many pages it is because I read it online and not a printed copy. But there is a Federal Register that accompanies the IDEA statute.

A Federal Register further explains the intent of the various parts of IDEA because putting that in the statute would be too long. The IDEA Federal Register is more than 600 pages long! No, I haven't read it cover to cover, but I've read more parts of it than I can count. (Tip: If you're reading IDEA and related documents online, you can use Control F if you don't already know because that is your key to finding words you want in IDEA or other regulations.)

Federal Statutes and the accompanying Federal Register are not written like summer beach-reads or bestsellers. They're dry and use clunky language that is difficult to get through. This is an obstacle for many parents to overcome, which I acknowledge. Still, it must be done.

For example, so often, parents will ask me, "What are my rights in the IEP process?" and that makes me sigh and want to roll my eyes. Every year, your school district gives you a copy of your Procedural Safeguards. For all of the things that schools forget to do, I find that this is not one of them.

The problem? The booklet is called "Procedural Safeguards." Ugh, how dry is that? Of course, no one knows that it's your parental rights and why no one wants to read it. The Procedural Safeguards booklet for my state is more than 50 pages long, and it's the smallest font you've ever seen. Of course there are no pictures or illustrations either. Just 50 pages of government-type speak that you have to read if you want to know your federally given rights.

Yuck. But I don't see that changing any time soon. That is one of the mantras that I tell my clients often. "Focus on what you can control." I cannot change IDEA or any of the booklets that go with it. But what I can control is my commitment to reading and learning it, no matter how difficult it may be.

Getting Used to All the Acronyms

Remember, it will get easier over time. Besides the parents' rights, another intimidating factor for parents is the frequent use of acronyms. Your use of acronyms will get better over time. And don't be afraid to ask the school staff to back up and tell you what it stands for. Many parents don't want to ask for help or explanation in an IEP meeting because they feel the lack of knowledge will make them appear vulnerable or "stupid" in the IEP process.

Many years ago, my husband and I bought our house. A few years later, we had an incident with our borough and the permission they gave to Fios to install cable. Our entire front property line was trashed. Not only did it look terrible, but every time it rained, it caused a giant muddy mess because they had not replaced the grass they tore up.

We were livid. I communicated several times to our borough council and the mayor. But here's the thing: I didn't know what I didn't know. And what I didn't know was anything about property easements. So, I was accusing lots of folks for doing things "illegally" which was incorrect. This made it very evident that I didn't know my rights, and it weakened my otherwise valid argument that they had destroyed part of our front yard. Nothing they had done was "illegal." It was just careless.

I see the word illegal get tossed around IEP issues a lot. Illegal generally refers to criminal statutes. IDEA and Section 504 are not criminal statutes. If they are not followed, there are no IEP police going around checking for compliance. No one will get arrested because of a failure to implement FAPE. The person has to violate a criminal law.

When you don't know the process, that is one thing. But when you repeat or state incorrect information, you're broadcasting to the team that you don't know the laws that protect your kids or our rights in the process. This can leave you open to being taken advantage of.

I understand the sense of urgency in wanting to get your child's issues fixed. But patience can be your friend. If you don't know something, a simple, "Let me think about this for a day or two and get back to you" is better than agreeing to something you don't agree with or trying to force an issue with incorrect information.

The IEP team is actually required to provide you with someone who can explain things to you, especially the evaluations. And there is no shame in not knowing an acronym or term that they use. Please don't be afraid to ask. After all, if they went to your workplace, I bet they wouldn't know what you're talking about either. IEP team members went to four years of school, often six or more. They do this day in and day out and have written hundreds of IEPs. Of course, they're going to rattle off acronyms and terms! It's second nature to them.

But don't be embarrassed if it's not second nature to you. It will be soon. And if you're truly not comfortable asking your team for help, my website has many in-depth resources and a message board for you to ask questions.

Know How Your State Laws Differ

IDEA is the federal law that governs IEPs, but one of the pillars of our government structure here in the United States is to "leave it up to the states." IDEA is no different. While IDEA says a lot about IEPs, it also leaves a lot up to the states to further define.

And it is up to the states to implement IEPs. The federal government plays no role in that and never will due to a 1970s law stating that education would always be implemented at the state level.

Knowing that specific law is not important for IEP advocacy. I mention it simply to explain why things are often very different from one state to another when it comes to IEPs. In this day and age of social media, IEP parents from all over the world (yes, military bases and US territories are included) can chat about IEPs. And things are often very different.

When it comes to states and their special education regulations, they can do more for the student than what IDEA calls for, but they cannot do less. As an example, IDEA states that all IEP students should be re-evaluated once every three years. Here in Pennsylvania, intellectually disabled students are re-evaluated every two years per our state law. Every two does more for the student than every three, so it's allowed. But Pennsylvania could not decide to re-evaluate once every five years. That would be less for the student.

IDEA states that school districts have 60 days to do an evaluation. Some states have backed that up to 30 or 45 days, which is more for the student. But a state cannot move it to 90 days.

Make sense? Whenever you are chatting with other IEP parents online, it's important to take everything with a grain of salt as they say. They may be correct but may live in a different state than you do.

Or they may just be wrong. I have seen some folks really dig their heels in and be extremely incorrect about something. I see this with parent to parent networking, and sometimes, it's the information coming from the school. I often refer to Dale Carnegie's 1936 book called *How to Win Friends and Influence People*.

Know How to Question People

One of his pieces of advice in that book is, "People do not like to be told that they are wrong."

Hoo boy! Did he ever nail that one, even a hundred years ago! He lists several studies and experiments where people said something incorrect and, even when shown an overwhelming amount of evidence to the contrary, refused to admit that they were wrong. Usually, at this point in one of my training sessions, a parent will raise a hand and say, "Well that's great. But sometimes, they really are wrong. So, then what?"

Yes, people are wrong. I point this out only because now that I am more aware of this and I am becoming more intentional about it, I have observed common behaviors related to this. And that is, you're not likely to "win friends and influence people," pun intended, by telling them that they are wrong. It immediately puts people on the defensive, can change the tone of an IEP meeting, and cause IEP team members to lose focus. Sometimes even the discussion gets off track.

I have encountered that scenario many times. When presented with a scenario where I am fairly sure the information is incorrect, even when it happens in an IEP meeting and the incorrect information is coming from school staff, I just flip it around. "Can you tell me where you found that? Do you have a link where it says that in our state regs? Because I've never heard this (Or, it is my understanding that... .) and I want to read up on it."

This allows people to save face a bit because, as I've found time and time again, just telling people, "That's incorrect, it's... ." is not likely to be met warmly.

Most school personnel believe they are serving your child and genuinely care about your child. There is a huge disconnect between what is taught to teachers when they are in college and what the IEP process really is like in day-to-day practice. Most school degrees focus on pedagogy and instruction, not the IEP process itself.

What ends up happening is that newer teachers or student teachers rely on the information given to them from their mentors. And they just accept it as fact. When you have special education directors or other administrators moving around from district to district to further their careers, bad information and bad practices can move around an entire state very quickly.

Very few IEP matters are truly urgent. So, take the time to look into it yourself.

Stay Focused on the Big Picture

One last concept in advocacy that I want to share with you, and please indulge me because it is important. I want to tell you a couple of scenarios involving parents and point out what is ineffective as far as advocacy.

I often do webinars and workshops for parent groups, churches, and the like. Together, with the event organizer, we pick a topic that is suited for this particular group. At the end of each one, I like to leave 15–20 minutes for an open Q&A. Over the years, I have found that this is a big draw to events like this: Parents love to talk about their IEPs and ask a "real advocate" their question. They'll even sit through my entire presentation, visibly bored or antsy, just waiting for me to stop talking so they can ask their very specific questions.

This one evening, this is exactly what happened. It was during the pandemic, and the pandemic was actually the topic of my presentation. If you remember, many kids lost out on services and other situations happened due to school closures, virtual learning, and so on. So, the presentation was a lot of "if then" scenarios pertaining to IEP services during the pandemic.

We get to the end of the presentation, and one mom starts telling us this story about her child's IEP not addressing all the child's needs and then some stories about some other boys at school and there were behavior situations and a few scuffles that resulted in disciplinary action, discipline reports, and incident reports.

At the end of all of this, this mom said, "And so I asked the school for the report, and they said that they don't have to give it to me. Do they have to give me this report?"

Now I don't want to scare anyone away from ever coming to hear me talk live or virtual, but I am a teacher and so I use these personal questions not just to help that specific person but also as a teachable moment.

So, I asked her, "Why do you need this report?"

Mom: "I just want to know if they have to give it to me because she said they didn't."
Me: "Right, I understand that. But why do you need it? What effect is it going to have on your child's progress or their IEP?"
Mom: "Well, I don't know, but aren't I entitled to this report?"
Me: "Probably, if it falls under FERPA (law that governs student records). But the information on this report, if you need information that's on it, is there another way you can glean this same information from something besides this report?"
Mom: "So, I should look up FERPA? What is FERPA?"

My goal is never to antagonize or embarrass people, but my attempt to get this parent to think critically failed miserably. Because she could not take her eye off of the (perceived) prize: the coveted report that school told her she couldn't have.

My observation after many years of doing advocacy is this: When parents don't know how to look at the big picture or know what to focus on, they find one little detail and focus on it. It's usually a black and white issue: It happened or it didn't.

They give her the report or they don't. They're legally obligated to give her the report or they aren't. It's concrete and measurable, which can feel like a life saver when you're drowning in abstract concepts like "appropriate education" and "meaningful progress."

I have done this myself. When Kevin was very small, I knew he wasn't making significant progress, but I didn't know what to do. I can't remember why I chose this option, but I chose to ask for twice the amount of OT he was receiving. At the time, he was receiving one hour a week of each: PT, OT, Speech, and education (a special ed teacher came to the house).

I went back and forth with our case manager. I was told things like "That's not our program model" and "If we do that, he'll be receiving more services than any other child in the county."

I persisted and finally I got it. One hour a week to two hours a week, wow! I doubled the amount of OT he was getting, and my kid was getting more services than any other kid in the entire county!

Looking back, I cringe and want to punch myself in the face. I didn't know what I didn't know. First of all, I live in a very large county with almost 800K people in it, so it's very unlikely that my child was receiving more services than anyone else. But that sure did feel like a win!

These are just some of the mistakes I made in that scenario:

1. The main one is that "I is for Individualized" piece; I let them even use reasons like "That's not our model" to deny me for a while.
2. I hadn't proven that Kevin needed another hour of OT, I just thought it would help.
3. I didn't look at the current services. Given his age at the time (toddler) and his profound autism, an hour of anything is too long. It likely would have been much more beneficial for him to have the same total amount of services, but each hour split into two sessions. I hadn't yet become an expert in my child, his diagnoses, and what was appropriate for him.
4. I let their evaluations drive the services without questioning them too much. He has other disabilities that were not addressed.

So, what happened? We got our extra hour of OT. I imagine back then I was expecting twice the progress, which didn't happen. I focused on one tangible thing that really didn't matter, but it was measurable. I didn't know what else to focus on, so I focused on that. He didn't make twice the progress, which left me with a lot of soul searching to do. I mean, why not? He was getting more services than any other kid in my county, right? How could he not be making meaningful progress.

It just so happened that around that same time, I was really digging in and learning all this IEP stuff and I figured it out. I got him a Functional Vision Assessment and an orientation and mobility (O&M) assessment. Shortly thereafter, he began receiving vision services from a TVI (teacher of the visually impaired) and O&M for him to better navigate his surroundings. I also advocated so our family priorities were considered when creating goals. As a result, his PT goals focused more on core strength for hypotonia and were much more practical and functional for his life. I advocated for an Independent Education Evaluation (IEE) for feeding/eating skills and so his OT and his speech language pathologist (SLP) were much better informed to help him.

It took many months of assessments and advocating, but once he had a solid IEP in place that was appropriate and meaningful for him, his progress took off.

Here are other examples I've run into:

*   A parent focusing on whether or not she got the IEP meeting invitation within the required time frame (if your state defines this)
*   Focusing on whether or not they got the final IEP to you within the required time frame (if your state defines this)
*   Focusing on whether or the child's evaluations were done in the 60 days required by IDEA or debating the school on whether it's calendar days or school days

I'm not suggesting that we let the schools off the hook for their responsibilities and timelines. But in the big picture, how much is this going to affect your child's outcomes if the evaluations are done within 65 days instead of 60? This is good information to have, but document it and move on. If you find yourself filing a complaint with your various complaint options, this will be good information as it may demonstrate a pattern of carelessness and disregard.

But in the moment, you've now taken the focus off of your child. And like the very first mom above, she was now arguing with her school about whether or not she should get that report she desired, and not even talking about the IEP anymore. If you're in an IEP meeting discussing that the personnel only gave you four days' notice for the meeting instead of their required 10 (check your state!), then you've completely changed the topic of conversation.

Document it and move on. Mindset matters in the IEP process. It's a large, overwhelming, confusing process with a lot of clunky words and language that we never use in other parts of our life.

That alone intimidates many parents from digging in and learning more. But a commitment to do a little bit each week will make you a better advocate. And it will reduce your urge to cling to small details that you understand but may not matter in the long run.

I understand wanting black and white, yes and no information. That certainly would make this easier. But while IDEA says a lot of things, the more you dig in, the more you'll find what it doesn't say. If you dig in and read parts of it from time to time, you'll find it to be surprisingly non-specific about a lot of things. I know this because I've looked for a lot of things when I was first starting out.

And since then, many parents have asked me, "Can you show me where it says... ." and "Can you tell me where it says..." because they're just so desperate for a fact or statement to cling to. And surely if they ask this well-known advocate (me!) this question, she'll know the answer and then I'll know what to point to, and my IEP team will be proven wrong, and voila! I get the IEP I want.

It doesn't work like that. Again, the laws are pretty non specific about much of this because everything is to be individualized to the child.

Focus on the Output

As you read your plays for this chapter, I want to leave you with one more tip as you become an advocate. That is, focus on output and not outcomes. What I mean by that is this–focus on what you are doing, as far as output toward being a better advocate. Not just focusing on the outcome of the meeting, or the outcome of your child. What have you read this month? What podcasts have you listened to, what webinars have you attended? What parts of your IEP have you read recently, or the progress monitoring reports?

Believe me: If you focus on what your output is toward those ultimate goals, the outcome will be achieved.

1. I must commit to learning the IEP process to be a better advocate for my child.
2. This will not get easier, but I will get better.
3. I will look for and commit to reading my Procedural Safeguards.
4. I will look for and bookmark my state's special education website and regulations on my computer.
5. I will not be afraid to ask for an explanation from school staff when I need it.

6. I will give myself grace for not knowing all the acronyms and will keep a cheat sheet in my binder when I attend IEP meetings.

7. People do not like to be told that they are wrong.

Your Play for This Chapter

Your play for this chapter is to look at your IEP, evaluation reports, and Procedural Safeguards. Make a note of what you don't understand. Put three checkboxes on each one.

☐ _____ Check this one when you've read the document and don't understand it.

☐ _____ Check this one when you've completed this book but still need further explanation.

☐ _____ Check this one when you looked online and read about this but still don't understand it.

Then take time to ask for help; there's no shame in that.

CHAPTER 2

Why Things Are the Way They Are

Before diving headfirst into all things individualized education program (IEP), it's important to take a step back and understand how we got here. The history of the Individuals with Disabilities Education Act (IDEA), which sets the framework for special education services in the United States, gives us much-needed perspective on why the IEP process can feel so contentious and adversarial.

The Early Days: The Horrors of Institutionalization

In the 1800s, disabled people were treated with a level of neglect and inhumanity that is almost unbearable to think about. Babies born with visible disabilities were often abandoned: left to die or sent to institutions that were more about warehousing people than caring for them. And for those with invisible disabilities or mental illness, the story wasn't much better. They were loaded onto wagons and sent to the next town or state, left to become someone else's "problem."

By the 1900s, we saw a slight shift but not enough to celebrate. Disabled babies were still taken from their families at birth. Parents were strongly encouraged, if not outright forced, to relinquish their children to institutions. These places were overcrowded, underfunded, and rife with abuse. Education was not part of the equation. Most children were warehoused with little to no stimulation or interaction.

In fact, in 1968, the exposé "Suffer the Little Children" aired on CBS and showed the gut-wrenching life inside the Pennhurst Asylum in Philadelphia. It was raw, shocking, and unforgettable. For many adults at the time, it was their first-ever view of what life was like for disabled people. It forced them to see what they'd previously ignored: institutionalized children living in filth, neglected, and abused.

I live near Pennhurst and have met former residents of Pennhurst. It did not fully close until 1987. It is estimated that thousands of people from Pennhurst are still alive today with many of them living on the streets or incarcerated. Pennhurst Longitudinal Study: **https:// aspe.hhs.gov/reports/pennhurst-longitudinal-study-combined-report-five-years-research-analysis-0**.

If you're curious (and brave enough), you can find "Suffer the Little Children" on YouTube. Fair warning: It's not for the faint of heart.

The Cases, Media, and Laws That Changed Everything

The outrage sparked by the Pennhurst exposé led to action. In 1971, a group of parents in Pennsylvania sued the state, arguing that their children deserved an education just like everyone else. The resulting Pennsylvania Association for Retarded Children (PARC) Decree laid the foundation for IDEA.

The PARC Decree refers to the agreement reached in the landmark case Pennsylvania Association for Retarded Children (PARC) v. Commonwealth of Pennsylvania in 1971. It was not a traditional court order following a trial but rather a consent decree, meaning a legally binding agreement both sides agreed to and approved by a federal judge.

The case was brought by families and advocates on behalf of 13 children with intellectual disabilities who had been denied access to public school under a Pennsylvania law that allowed schools to exclude children who hadn't reached the "mental age of 5" (remember Billy?).

The PARC case—and its decree—*directly influenced* the creation of Public Law 94-142, passed in 1975 and now known as the Individuals with Disabilities Education Act (IDEA). Here's how:

- **Free Appropriate Public Education (FAPE):** The PARC Decree established that all children deserve a public education, which became IDEA's cornerstone.
- **Individualized Education:** The idea that instruction must meet the student's unique needs began with PARC.
- **Parent Rights and Due Process:** IDEA's procedural safeguards were modeled after what was put in place in PARC and a few similar cases.
- **Inclusion and Least Restrictive Environment (LRE):** The idea that kids should not be segregated unnecessarily comes straight from this ruling. This would be reinforced and further defined in 1980s by the US Supreme Court. Until then, schools mostly kept disabled children in separate classrooms or separate buildings even though the law said otherwise.

Meanwhile, another exposé hit the airwaves in 1972, and it got much more attention than the 1968 documentary. Geraldo Rivera's "Willowbrook: The Last Great Disgrace" shined a light on atrocities at the Willowbrook State School in New York, similar to the situation at Pennhurst near Philadelphia. Rivera's storytelling skills brought even more national attention to the plight of institutionalized children, pushing the issue further into the public consciousness.

Shortly after PARC, the Mills vs Board of Education 1972 case extended this principle to children with a broader range of disabilities, including behavioral and emotional challenges. The District of Columbia had been excluding children from school due to the cost of accommodations, and Mills argued that doing so violated their constitutional rights. The court ruled that lack of funds was not a valid excuse to deny children an education. This case reinforced the idea that *all* children have a right to an education, and that schools must provide it equitably.

These court cases, coupled with growing public awareness, led to a wave of legal and legislative change.

These cases, along with the horrifying revelations from institutions like Willowbrook and Pennhurst (amplified by documentaries like "Suffer the Little Children"), shifted public awareness. For the first time, the general public saw children with disabilities not as burdens or tragedies but as people with potential who had been systematically excluded. The legal system began to affirm that exclusion and neglect were not just unethical: They were unconstitutional.

Together, these cases formed the legal and moral foundation for IDEA. They established that education is a right, not a privilege, and that disability could no longer be used as a reason to deny access to public schools. IDEA would go on to require that all children with disabilities receive a Free Appropriate Public Education (FAPE) in the Least Restrictive Environment (LRE)—terms we now see in every IEP.

The Rehabilitation Act of 1973 was passed two years before IDEA. This act does not provide special education, but Section 504 provides access to accommodations for disabled people and includes schools. Section 504 was in place in 1973 but was rarely followed. This would lead to the famous 1977 protests of Section 504, or the "Section 504 Sit Ins."

Section 504 is about access and equity. It was intended to be broad and inclusive and enforce civil rights protections for individuals with disabilities in any federally funded setting, including schools. But let's be clear: This didn't happen without resistance. Schools worried about the cost, and those concerns haven't gone away. While Section 504 was passed in 1973, it wasn't enforced with fidelity until 1977 and after.

IDEA was first introduced in early 1975. As IDEA was moving through Congress, *One Flew Over the Cuckoo's Nest* was released and showed insight into life in a mental institution. We still have a long way to go in how we treat disabled and mentally ill people, but there's no denying that these events helped change perceptions.

All of these things put together—awareness from TV programs, Section 504 seeing increased litigation and protests, and pending court cases—led to the Education for All Handicapped Children Act, which created the foundation of IDEA. In November of 1975, President Ford signed IDEA into law. In 1975, Congress passed Public Law 94-142, known then as the Education for All Handicapped Children Act, which is the law we now call the Individuals with Disabilities Education Act (IDEA). This landmark legislation was created in response to growing public pressure, media exposure of institutional abuse, and a wave of court cases affirming the rights of students with disabilities.

Before the law, more than a million children were being denied access to public education entirely, and millions more were sitting in classrooms without support or services.

IDEA changed that. For the first time in U.S. history, the federal government required schools to provide a Free Appropriate Public Education (FAPE) to every child with a disability, in the Least Restrictive Environment (LRE) possible.

The law was more than a policy shift. It was a civil rights milestone that recognized students with disabilities as full members of the public education system.

But not everything has been smooth for IEPs since then. Just a few years later, from 1980 to 1984, the Reagan administration worked to weaken the Education for all Handicapped Children Act. When it wasn't successful, the Reagan Administration terminated the Social Security benefits of hundreds of thousands of disabled recipients.

Back then, when IDEA 1975 was passed, Congress made a promise to fund "up to 40%" of the costs associated with IDEA. The law authorized the federal government to fund up to 40% of the average per-pupil expenditure to help states cover the additional costs of educating students with disabilities.

This is often referred to as the "full funding promise." It was authorized, not mandated. That meant Congress gave itself permission to fund up to 40%, but didn't actually require itself to do so. As a result, actual federal funding has never come close to the promised level. In most years since 1975, the federal government has funded only about 10–15% of special education costs, leaving states and local districts to cover the rest.

In other words, IDEA is an unfunded mandate, leaving schools to scramble for resources.

Then, in 1990, the Americans with Disabilities Act (ADA) was passed. This was another game-changer, but again, it has been an unfunded mandate. And like IDEA, it's a complaint-based law. In other words, if a building isn't accessible, it's assumed to be fine unless someone files a complaint

IDEA is also complaint-based. Unless parents uses their parental rights in the IEP process and files an official complaint, it is assumed that things are fine. But since you are reading this book, your IEP is probably not fine. There's an entire cottage industry built up to support Parent vs. School IEP Disputes; attorneys, advocates, training, agencies, and experts. The necessity of this parental support indicates that things are not fine with IDEA.

The Problem with Unfunded Mandates

As you can see, disability rights laws are relatively new, and most were passed within the last 50 years. It is not lost on me that if my son was born a generation earlier, I'd have been strongly encouraged to institutionalize him. This is also why stigma and bias against disabled students still linger and why parents often feel like they're fighting an uphill battle. People believe that some kids are "uneducable" or that disabled students must be in separate classrooms or buildings.

It's also why there's no IEP police force swooping in to ensure compliance. The burden falls on parents to advocate, document, and, when necessary, file complaints.

Here's the big question: Why is the IEP process so frustrating? The answer boils down to money. Schools don't have enough of it. IDEA funding is woefully inadequate, and the costs often fall to local taxpayers.

In Pennsylvania, for example, public charter schools aren't even required to spend their special education funding on IEP students. That's resulted in millions of dollars being diverted to unrelated expenses. It's infuriating, but it's the system we have. One cyber charter school in Pennsylvania spent $4 million on gift cards to students in one year! **https://edvoterspa.org/cyber-charter-waste-of-the-week/**.

And let's be real: When schools push back against parents, it's rarely about what's best for the child. It's about protecting budgets.

So, what can we do? First, let's stop asking "why." Why is the system this way? Why do schools act like this? The answer is money. Let's move on.

Moving Forward

The Individuals with Disabilities Education Act (IDEA) is the cornerstone of special education in the United States. It was first passed in 1975 and revised several times since (1990 and 2004). It ensures that children with disabilities are provided with Free Appropriate Public Education (FAPE) tailored to their unique needs. This legislation isn't just about access to education; it's about ensuring meaningful progress in the LRE possible.

For parents, IDEA can feel like a double-edged sword. On one hand, it offers rights and protections to children and families. On the other, understanding those rights and using them effectively can feel like trying to read a foreign language without a translator. Many parents enter the process trusting the school system will take care of the issues their child has only to realize later that advocacy is essential to ensure their child truly benefits from what IDEA promises. At the heart of IDEA are six guiding principles that shape how special education services are delivered in the United States. These principles aren't just abstract legal concepts; they're the foundation of every IEP meeting, every support decision, and every parent's right to be involved. Together, they ensure that students with disabilities are not only included in public education but are also given the opportunity to succeed with meaningful supports. Understanding these six principles will help you better navigate the IEP process and advocate more effectively for your child. The six principles of IDEA as we commonly refer to them today were not written word-for-word in the original IDEA legislation. Instead, they are a framework developed by educators, legal scholars, and policy experts to help summarize and explain the key rights and protections embedded throughout the law.

This chapter will explore these six principles, connect them to the IEP process, and as always, give you the tools to advocate effectively for your child.

Free Appropriate Public Education (FAPE)

Every child with a disability is entitled to a FAPE, which ensures that services provided by the school meet the unique needs of your child at no cost to you. Here's the key word: appropriate. It doesn't mean the best education, but it does mean one that enables your children to make progress in light of their circumstances. FAPE is the cornerstone of IDEA: It's why IEPs exist.

Here's how it relates to the IEP: The IEP is the document that ensures FAPE is delivered. When you're at the table, ask yourself these questions: Does this IEP enable my child to progress? Are the services and supports in place sufficient to meet their needs? For example, if your child struggles with reading, are there goals and interventions designed to address their specific deficits, such as decoding or comprehension? If not, the IEP might not meet the standard for FAPE, and you'll need to push back.

Appropriate Evaluation

This principle mandates that schools conduct thorough and accurate evaluations of your child's needs. It's not just about testing; it's about ensuring evaluations use reliable methods, consider multiple sources of information, and avoid bias.

Here's how it relates to the IEP: The results of evaluations drive everything on the IEP. Evaluations determine eligibility, establish baselines for goals, and help identify the services your child needs. If the school refuses to evaluate in an area of suspected need— let's say, executive functioning skills or sensory processing—you have the right to request it. You can also request an Independent Educational Evaluation (IEE) if you disagree with the school's findings. Without appropriate evaluations, your child's IEP could be a house of cards, built on shaky ground.

Individualized Education Program (IEP)

The IEP itself is one of IDEA's six principles. It's not just paperwork (though it can sure feel like that sometimes); it's a legally binding document. The IEP outlines your child's present levels of performance, annual goals, services, accommodations, and more. It's the road map for how the school will support your child.

Here's how it relates to the IEP: This one is obvious, right? But here's what's not so obvious: Every part of the IEP should be *specific* and *measurable*. Vague goals like "will improve math skills" don't cut it. You want to see something like, "By the end of the IEP year, Jane will correctly solve two-step word problems involving addition and subtraction with 80% accuracy in four out of five trials." It's also critical that services and supports align with your child's needs. If evaluations indicate a speech delay, where are the speech therapy hours? If the school writes up a generic IEP, it's not fulfilling this principle.

Least Restrictive Environment (LRE)

The LRE principle states that children with disabilities should be educated with their non-disabled peers to the greatest extent appropriate. This doesn't mean "mainstreaming" at all costs; it means finding the right balance between inclusion and specialized support.

Here's how it relates to the IEP: When discussing placement, the IEP team must consider whether your child can be successful with appropriate supports in a general education classroom. For example, a student with sensory needs might thrive with noise-canceling headphones and movement breaks instead of being placed in a separate classroom. However, if the general education setting isn't working despite accommodations, a more restrictive setting might be needed

On one hand, you want your children to be included to learn alongside their peers, to be part of the school community. On the other hand, you worry: *Will they get the support they need? Will they be safe? Will they be accepted?* LRE isn't just a legal requirement; it's an emotional decision point, and every parent wants to get it right. It's not about choosing more less inclusion; it's about what's truly appropriate for your child.

Parent Participation

IDEA guarantees that parents have a voice in their child's education. You're not just allowed to participate in the IEP process; instead, you're a critical member of the team.

How it relates to the IEP: This principle gives you the right to provide input, ask questions, and even disagree with the rest of the team. If the school proposes removing a service, you can—and should—ask for the data supporting that decision. If you feel the IEP isn't addressing all of your child's needs, ask for revisions. Don't be afraid to bring an advocate or other support person to meetings. Remember, no changes can be made to the IEP without your consent.

Procedural Safeguards

Procedural Safeguards are the rights that protect you and your child throughout the IEP process. They ensure you're informed, involved, and able to dispute decisions if necessary.

How it relates to the IEP: Procedural Safeguards cover everything from receiving written notices of proposed changes to your child's IEP to your right to file a due process complaint if you believe your child's rights are being violated. Knowing these safeguards is your armor in the IEP process. For instance, if the school refuses to provide a service, you can request Prior Written Notice (PWN), which forces them to explain their reasoning in writing. This can be a game-changer when escalating concerns.

Putting IDEA to Work

Each of these six principles isn't just a legal requirement; they're tools you can use to advocate effectively for your child. When you walk into an IEP meeting, bring these principles with you. Use them to ask questions like:

- Does this IEP provide FAPE? Are the services sufficient to meet my child's unique needs?
- Were evaluations thorough and appropriate? Did they assess all areas of suspected need?
- Is the IEP specific, measurable, and tailored to my child?

- Is the placement decision based on the LRE?
- Am I being included as an equal partner in this process?
- Are Procedural Safeguards being upheld?

Understanding these principles doesn't just make you a better advocate: It empowers you to hold the school accountable. Because at the end of the day, this isn't just about compliance. It's about ensuring your child gets the education and opportunities they deserve. And if the IEP process feels like wading through molasses, these principles can help you find solid ground.

So, grab your IEP binder, sharpen your pencils, and grab coffee or water to hydrate. You've got this.

Your Play for This Chapter

Grab your child's IEP and evaluation report(s). Keep them close to this book because trust me: You'll read something and want to see what your IEP says!

CHAPTER 3

What Is an IEP?

An individualized education program (IEP) is a legally binding document designed to meet the unique educational needs of a child with disabilities. Governed by the Individuals with Disabilities Education Act (IDEA), an IEP provides a road map of supports, accommodations, and specialized instruction to ensure a child has access to a Free Appropriate Public Education (FAPE).

Some states, mine included, use the word *plan* instead of *program* in their language; the two can be used interchangeably. In other words, an IEP plan is the same as an IEP program.

If your child gets an IEP, it is essential for you as a parent to be familiar with both the federal and state regulations for IEPs and be an active participant in the entire process. Otherwise, you're at risk for your child not receiving the education and services they are entitled to.

An IEP isn't just a school document: It's a process, a commitment, and sometimes, a lifeline for families whose kids need help. So, let's start from the beginning and break this down.

Advocacy Tip: I cover parental rights later in this book. But I'll say it here first: It's up to you, as the parent, to read your rights booklet and to ask for help when you need it. Schools are legally obligated to explain to you what you don't understand. Your school team is not going to beg you to learn and exercise your rights; instead, you must take ownership of this.

What Exactly Is an IEP?

An IEP is a detailed document that outlines a child's current academic and functional performance, sets measurable goals, and lists the services the school will provide. Think of it as a contract between you and the school: It specifies what the school will do, how it will do it, and how it will measure progress.

When students have an IEP, it means they are eligible to receive special education. To receive special education, you must have an IEP.

Specifically, the IEP document details what type and frequency of Special Education Supports and Related Services your child will receive. The supports are defined by a federal statute called IDEA, but it is your local school district that develops and implements an IEP. Like many other American laws, Congress creates and passes the statute but "leaves it up to the states" as far as implementation.

The IEP age range is 3–21. Prior to age three, children get an Individualized Family Service Plan (IFSP). It's a legal document used in early intervention services for children from birth to age three who have developmental delays or disabilities. Unlike an IEP, an IFSP focuses not just on the child's needs but also on the family's needs in supporting their child's development.

To get an IEP, your school team of evaluators must have evaluated your children and found them to be eligible under one of the IDEA 13 Categories of Disability (covered in Chapter 6).

(Note that whether or not you refer to your child as "disabled" is up to you and your child.) Here's what an IEP typically includes:

- **Present Levels of Performance:** How your child is doing right now.
- **Goals:** Specific, measurable objectives to help your child make progress.
- **Services:** Things like speech therapy, occupational therapy, or specialized instruction.
- **Accommodations/Modifications:** Tools to help your child access the curriculum, such as extended time or a quiet testing area.
- **Progress Monitoring:** How and when you'll be informed about progress.

The key purposes of an IEP are:

- **To identify the student's strengths and needs:** The IEP team, which includes parents/guardians, teachers, and other professionals, assesses the student's current level of performance and identifies their strengths and needs.
- **To set academic and functional goals:** Based on the student's strengths and needs, the IEP team sets measurable goals for the student to achieve in the academic and functional areas.
- **To provide specialized instruction and related services:** The IEP specifies the specialized instruction, accommodations, modifications, and related services (such as speech therapy or occupational therapy) that students require to achieve their goals.
- **To ensure access to the general education curriculum:** The IEP team determines how the student can participate in the general education curriculum with appropriate accommodations and modifications.
- **To monitor progress and adjust goals:** The IEP includes a plan to monitor the student's progress and make adjustments to the goals and services provided as needed to ensure continued progress.

An IEP is designed to ensure that students with disabilities receive a free and appropriate public education that meets their unique needs and prepares them for further education, employment, and independent living.

If you're thinking, *Wow, that sounds like a lot of legal and educational jargon*, you're right. That's why understanding the process—and getting help when you need it—is so critical. As someone who has been navigating IEP meetings for more than 15 years, I can tell you that being on the learning curve can be frustrating and tiring. All those phrases, acronyms, and principles can be overwhelming at times, but that's what this book aims to clarify. If you are confused or don't know a term, there is a glossary in Appendix A.

When Should You Get an IEP?

IEPs are for children who meet these two criteria under the IDEA:

1. They have a qualifying disability that affects their learning. This includes a range of conditions from autism and ADHD to visual impairments and developmental delays.
2. They need specialized instruction to make progress in school.

   Here are some signs that your child might need an IEP:

   - Struggles with academic skills
   - Speech or language delays
   - Social or emotional difficulties
   - Behavioral challenges
   - Attention and focus issues
   - Sensory processing issues
   - Delays in motor skills
   - Medical or developmental diagnoses

IEPs are living documents and must be reviewed annually, but they can be adjusted or changed at any time. For example:

- When a children's needs change, their performance may change; this could be due to a new condition, trauma in the household, or because previous adjustments to the IEP are not working
- If the environment changes, such as moving to a different classroom or different school building
- If academic or social demands change
- Any time you see significant progress or regression in a short period of time in any domain (academic, behavioral), you should revisit the IEP

What to Do If You're Told Your Child Needs an IEP

An IEP can be initiated by either the parent or the school. If parents suspect their child may have a disability that impacts learning, they have the right to request an evaluation in writing. Similarly, a teacher or other school staff member who notices a child struggling academically, behaviorally, or socially can also refer the student for evaluation. In either case, the referral sets the special education process in motion and must be followed by a timely response from the school. The key point is this: Parents, teachers, counselors, and other school personnel can all make referrals when there is concern that a student may need special education services.

So, the school calls you in, and someone says, "We think your child should receive special education evaluations." What now?

1. **Evaluations:** You can't start an IEP without assessments. The school will conduct tests to determine your child's eligibility under IDEA. These could include academic assessments, psychological evaluations, or observations.

   - Advocacy tip: *Always* ask for copies of the evaluation reports before the meeting so you can review them. IEP evaluation reports are long and often complex documents, full of data, numbers, and unfamiliar words. Best practice is to read it beforehand with sticky notes and a highlighter so you have your questions prepared. If an advance copy is not made available to you, you can always ask for another meeting with the school psychologist. Per the IDEA, the school is required to provide parents with a staff person who can explain these reports to parents.

2. **Learn the Terminology:** You'll hear terms like LRE, FAPE, and PLOP. It's okay to ask for clarification. And if you feel like you need an IEP Glossary, see Appendix A. I'll also define terms as we move through the book.

3. **Gather Your Information:** Bring anything you think is relevant, e.g., private evaluations, work samples.

4. **Keep Communication Written:** This is my mantra. You want everything documented. If it's not in writing, it didn't happen.

5. **Stay Calm, but Don't Be a Doormat:** Remember, you're part of the team. If you feel steamrolled, hit pause. You can always reschedule a meeting to gather your thoughts.

The IEP process can feel like an emotional rollercoaster. One minute, you're hopeful that this will finally help your child; the next, you're ready to scream because the school's data doesn't match what you see at home. Here's how to approach it:

- **Be Prepared:** Have an agenda, questions, and goals for every meeting.
- **Think Long-Term:** The goal isn't just to make it through this year. It's to equip your child for life.
- **Lean on Resources:** There's no shame in asking for help. Whether it's joining my online community, hiring an advocate, or using my IEP Toolkit, you don't have to do this alone.

What an IEP Can (and Can't) Do for Your Child

An IEP is a powerful tool, but it's not a magic wand. While it can open the door to essential supports and services, it won't fix every struggle.

An IEP can:

- Provide specialized instruction tailored to your child's needs.
- Ensure access to the general education curriculum with accommodations.
- Set measurable goals for academic and functional skills.
- Protect your child's rights under federal law.

What an IEP *can't* do:

- Guarantee progress. (Sorry, but IEPs aren't perfect.)
- Prevent all conflicts. You'll likely have to advocate, sometimes fiercely.

When to Seek Assistance

The IEP process can feel like navigating a foreign country where you don't speak the language. I hope to change much of that for you with this book. But here are some times when you need backup:

- **If you feel stuck:** You've been to meeting after meeting, but nothing's changing.
- **If the school says no:** Whether it's to services, evaluations, or accommodations, don't accept "no" as the final answer.
- **If you're overwhelmed:** Advocacy is exhausting. Let someone else carry the load. An advocate can help you navigate the system, ensure compliance, and save your sanity.

IEPs are important because they help to level the playing field for students with disabilities. Without an IEP, students with disabilities may struggle to keep up with their classmates and may not receive the support they need to succeed.

Your Play for This Chapter

Mentally commit to both finishing this book and promising yourself that you'll learn this IEP stuff to the best of your ability. As I said earlier in this chapter, being on the learning curve is tiring, so rest when you need to. But the IEP process never gets easier (sorry!). You get better.

CHAPTER 4

What Can I Ask for on an IEP?

I t might seem a little bit of "putting the cart before the horse" by putting this chapter so early in the book and before the chapter on evaluations. This is on purpose.

"What can I ask for on my child's individualized education program (IEP)?" is hands down one of the most common questions I get from parents. And I want to temper expectations around this question. Because if you're new to IEPs, you might think, "Yay! An IEP for my child! Now I can ask for anything." Or maybe you're into this a few years already, and you've asked for many things and cannot figure out why you're always told no.

I totally get it. The IEP process can feel like walking into a restaurant where everyone else seems to know the secret menu, and you're stuck wondering what you're allowed to order.

My answer? You can ask for anything. I mean it. You truly can ask for anything. The real trick isn't in the asking but in understanding how to support your ask with data and documentation. Because the caveat is: You can ask for anything as long as you can demonstrate that it is Free and Appropriate Education (FAPE) for your child.

Many parents aren't aware of how important it is to learn the IEP process, and it can be frustrating when things don't go as expected. But once you understand how it all works, you can advocate more effectively and see better results. Remember, we were all drafted on to a team we never asked to be on. But we either learn to play the game and win, or we don't. The choice is ours.

For perspective, remember that the Individuals with Disabilities Education Act (IDEA) mandates that the school provide you with someone who can explain your child's IEP evaluations to you. And as part of IDEA, every state is required to have a Parent Training Information Center to help parents understand IEPs and the IEP process. Those who wrote IDEA acknowledge that most parents will not know this the first time they encounter it.

The Myth of the IEP Process

First, let's bust a common myth. Many parents come into the IEP process with the assumption that there's a standard list of services, supports, and placements to choose from. They imagine there's some kind of hidden menu that schools keep tucked away, and their job is to figure out how to unlock it.

But IDEA doesn't work that way. Its whole point is to prevent cookie-cutter solutions. IEPs must be individualized. No two children are the same even if they share a diagnosis, so no two IEPs should look the same either.

Let's put it another way: Imagine walking into a shoe store. Instead of offering dozens of sizes and styles, the store only carries one size. Even if the shoes are beautiful and high-quality, they're useless if they don't fit your feet. That's what IDEA is trying to avoid. It ensures that schools don't offer "one-size-fits-all" solutions but instead provide supports tailored to your child's unique needs.

So, there's no magical list of services because the law forbids it. What you can ask for depends entirely on what your child needs as identified through evaluations, assessments, and observations. Examples include:

- Specialized instruction (e.g., direct reading instruction, small-group math support)
- Related services (e.g., speech therapy, occupational therapy, counseling)
- Accommodations (e.g., extended time, preferential seating, noise-canceling headphones)
- Assistive technology (e.g., communication devices, text-to-speech software)
- Behavioral supports (e.g., a Functional Behavior Assessment, a Behavior Intervention Plan)
- Transition planning (e.g., life skills training, job coaching, vocational assessments)

Well, it looks like I have created a list of what you can ask for, and there is a more specific one in Appendix I for all kinds of learning disabilities and skill deficiencies. My point here is that I would never expect your IEP team to hand you such a list and say, "Here's a list, tell us which ones you think he needs."

That would be too limiting and would violate the main principle of IDEA, which is individualized. The key isn't what to ask for; it's being able to demonstrate that your child requires it.

Evaluations: The Starting Point

Every single thing on your child's IEP should flow from one source: evaluations. These are the foundation of the entire process.

Evaluations identify your child's strengths, challenges, and needs. They provide the data that drive goals, services, and placements. How to request IEP evaluations for your child is in the next chapter.

Here's the sequence:

1. Evaluations identify needs.
2. Needs inform goals.
3. Goals determine the supports and services necessary to achieve them.
4. Supports and services guide placement.

This sequence is critical. Skipping a step—or trying to rearrange the order—can lead to confusion, frustration, and missed opportunities for your child.

Building Your Case: Data and Documentation

You need data to back up your requests. It's not enough to say, "I think my child would benefit from social skills instruction." You need to show the IEP team why it's necessary.

- **Examples of Data and Documentation Evaluations:** Does your child's speech-language evaluation show deficits in pragmatic language? That's your evidence for social skills instruction.
- **Teacher Input:** Does your child's teacher report difficulties with peer interactions? That supports your request, too.
- **Observations:** Have you noticed struggles during playdates or group activities? Your perspective matters.

    The more evidence you can provide, the stronger your case.

The "Ask for the Moon" Mindset

Let me pause here to emphasize something: You don't have to censor yourself when advocating for your child.

Too often, parents hesitate to ask for what their child really needs. They're afraid of being seen as "demanding" or "unreasonable." But here's the truth: Schools don't grant services out of generosity—they grant them because they're legally required to provide a FAPE.

FAPE means your children have the right to supports and services that meet their unique needs. If those needs require something unconventional or expensive, that's not your problem to solve. It's the school's job to figure out how to provide it.

So, go ahead and ask for the moon. If the data back you up, the law is on your side.

Advocacy Tip: You can't add supports or services to the IEP unless there's a goal tied to it.

Let's say you want your child to receive occupational therapy for handwriting. Before that can happen, the IEP must include a goal for improving handwriting. And before that goal can exist, the evaluations must show that handwriting is an area of need.

This is why it's so important to review your child's evaluations carefully. Make sure they accurately capture all of your child's challenges. If something is missing—like fine motor skills, social skills, or emotional regulation—speak up. You can request additional assessments or independent evaluations if needed.

Steps of the IEP Process:
IDEA has defined a specific process for IEPs.

- Identification or referral (parent or teacher)
- Parental consent for evaluations
- Evaluation
- Eligibility determination

- IEP meeting is scheduled
- IEP is developed: This includes, the goals, supports and interventions and placement
- Parental consent for services
- IEP services begin
- Progress monitoring
- Annual review
- Reevaluation (at least every three years)

Placement: The Final Step of IEP Development

Placement is sometimes the most contentious part of the IEP process. But here's what you need to remember: Placement is the last step of IEP development, not the first. In my experience, parents look to pick a placement first. And that's natural and understandable because you want to visualize what your child's day is going to look like. But that's not how the process works when writing an IEP.

The IEP team doesn't start by choosing a placement and then building an IEP around it. Instead, they build the IEP first—identifying the child's needs, setting goals, and determining supports—and then select the placement that can best deliver those supports.

If the IEP is the recipe, placement is the kitchen where it's cooked.

Common Pitfalls to Avoid

Let's talk about five common mistakes parents make and how to avoid them:

1. Skipping the Evaluation Step: If you don't have data to back up your requests, the school can (and likely will) deny them.
2. Focusing Solely on Placement: Don't get hung up on where your child will be placed. Focus on building a strong IEP first.
3. Failing to Document: Always put your requests in writing. Keep copies of emails, letters, and meeting notes.
4. Accepting Vague Language: Push for specificity. "Will receive support in math" is too vague. "Will receive 30 minutes of direct math instruction, three times per week, in a one-to-one setting" is much better.
5. Not Using Your Rights: If you disagree with the team's decisions, remember that you have options: Mediation, due process, and state complaints are all tools you can use.

Following the Process: Example

To illustrate the power of following the process, let me share a real-life example:

I worked with a family whose child struggled with severe anxiety. The school initially dismissed the parents' concerns, saying, "He seems fine here." But the parents persisted. They provided documentation from a private therapist, data from an independent evaluation, and detailed observations from home.

Because they followed the process—gathering data, documenting needs, and advocating effectively—their child's IEP was updated to include counseling services, a sensory-friendly workspace, and a modified schedule to reduce stress. Within months, his anxiety decreased, and his academic performance improved.

Free and Appropriate Public Education (FAPE)

Finally, when you want to know what you can ask for, you need to be familiar with the FAPE guidelines. With IDEA, our kids are guaranteed a FAPE, and the IEP team decides what FAPE is for each child. You are a mandated member of the IEP team.

Remember when I said that you have to not only become an expert in IEPs but also concerning your child's condition as well? This is why. If you are agreeing to your child's IEP on paper, regardless of how you feel about it mentally, you are agreeing that IEP is FAPE for your child. If you don't really agree with it, you are letting the rest of the IEP team define FAPE for your child.

So, you have to take a step back and learn what works for students with your child's learning disabilities and get it all documented on paper. Many parents get "frozen" in this step. They know that their child's IEP isn't appropriate, isn't enough, and/or their child isn't making progress or may even be regressing. They just don't know how to get out of this situation. They may be networking with other parents and see these "pie in the sky" lists of interventions that they are certain will work for their child, but the team always says no.

You have to back up everything with data and documentation. You need to not only demonstrate how that specific intervention will work for your child but also demonstrate that what the child is currently receiving is not working.

"Well, they're the school! Certainly they see this! Why can't they do it?!?!"

I don't know the answer to that question. They came to the table with their offer of FAPE, and since you didn't exercise your parental rights to disagree with it, the team assumes that you agree this is FAPE for your child. Why would they come to any other conclusion?

Another situation that I encounter is that parents experience the situation I just described above: They don't think this IEP is enough, but they agree with it because they don't know what else to do. They leave the IEP meeting with all kinds of emotions: mad, sad, frustrated, despondent. But a few days or weeks after the meeting, those emotions fade and all involved get back into their routines.

Those feelings are forgotten, and the parent has hope that the next meeting will be better. I've asked parents this: "Why are you expecting them to come to the table next time with a different offer?" You agreed that this is FAPE for your child. They think you agree. The team is not going to suddenly change course and come up with an entirely different set of interventions if it thinks you agree with this one.

FAPE. Learn it, live it, embrace it. It's essential that you become an expert in your child's condition and the concept of FAPE and be able to document what FAPE is for your child. Otherwise, you're facing a lifetime of IEPs that give you that uneasy feeling in the pit of your stomach.

Your Play for This Chapter

Make a wish list of IEP supports and services for your children that are not on their current IEP. Future chapters will give more information about this, but as you're reading, think about whether or not you have the documentation to support asking for this.

CHAPTER 5

How to Request IEP Evaluations

I f your children don't have an individualized education program (IEP) yet but you believe they need one, let me start by congratulating you. No, really: I mean it. You're ahead of the curve. Most parents don't start looking for information until they're deep into the IEP process or, worse, after things have already gone downhill. So, give yourself a pat on the back for being proactive and taking this first step.

Now let's talk about how to get an IEP. Spoiler alert: You don't actually ask for an IEP. That might sound counterintuitive, but stay with me. IEPs are developed based on data collected from educational evaluations. So, what you're really asking for is an evaluation. Everything else—goals, supports, services—flows from the results of that evaluation.

The First Step: Requesting an Evaluation

Your request for an evaluation should always be in writing. This creates a paper trail, which is critical if there are delays or disagreements down the road. Many parents wonder if they should start with a phone call or email. While it's fine to have a preliminary discussion with your child's teacher, the official request must be written to protect your rights.

What Evaluations to Request

Many parents ask, *What should I even request?* Or, *what if I want to request specific IEP evaluations?*

I don't recommend asking for specific assessments. The school is required to evaluate in every area of suspected disability. I would just make sure that you have listed every concern. I personally feel that if you request specific evaluations, it weakens your case should you want to request an Independent Educational Evaluation (IEE): more on IEEs below. The school could then deny your request for an IEE, saying, "Well, we did the evaluations you asked for."

Additionally, we're not professional educators. We don't know test protocols. You don't know if they have someone qualified to do that exam. Is that assessment even calibrated for all populations? There are too many variables for my comfort. Stick to what parents are good at, which is identifying the struggles you see.

You want to make sure your children are tested in the areas of their skill deficits. For example, if you suspect a visual deficit, any evaluation that tests for processing, reading, writing (if it's not a visual assessment) and you will not know if it was an accurate assessment. Does that make sense? Also, when you get your results, read the reports carefully and determine if you got all the answers you were looking for.

That said, here's a list of common evaluations, depending on your child's challenges:

- Psychoeducational Evaluation: Measures cognitive abilities, learning styles, and academic achievement.
- Speech-Language Evaluation: Assesses speech, language comprehension, and communication skills.
- Occupational Therapy (OT) Evaluation: Evaluates fine motor skills, sensory needs, and self-help abilities.
- Functional Behavioral Assessment (FBA): Identifies triggers for challenging behaviors and develops strategies to address them.
- Assistive Technology Assessment: Determines if tools like communication devices or apps could help your child.
- Social/Emotional Evaluation: Looks at anxiety, ADHD, autism, and other emotional factors affecting learning.

Ask for comprehensive evaluations. I have a chart with more evaluations in this book.

Schools often try to get by with the minimum (hello, budget cuts!), but you are allowed to request more if you suspect other areas of need.

What to Include in Your Request

When drafting your letter, include specific examples of the challenges your child is facing. These examples help the school understand why you're making the request and provide context for the evaluation.

- Get everything in writing. Everything. Start now, get in the habit of writing and documenting everything. Your first step is going to be to send a written request. My advice would be to send it to the school principal with your child's teacher getting a copy of it. CC them on it.
- Be very clear about what you are requesting. State this very clearly: I wish to have my child evaluated for special education services or accommodations. *No gray areas*. Not "Hey, I think she's struggling in school. Is there something we can do?" Direct request. If you do otherwise, it will only drag out the process.

- If you're not positive your child needs special education, there are other options. Maybe you're not quite ready to request special education services. Still, be clear about what you want. Ask to meet about a Response to Intervention (RTI) and ask them to explain that process to you. Go over it, go home and read about it, and then make your decision.

- Describe exactly what you are seeing. You want to be clear. What reading struggles are you seeing? Concerning social skills, time management, and whatever skill deficits you are seeing, describe them in bullet points in this letter.

- Be Specific: Instead of saying "He struggles in school," try "He cannot independently complete assignments that involve more than one step." Specific examples make your case stronger.

- Should I ask for specific IEP tests and IEP evaluations? No. There are thousands upon thousands of different types of educational assessments. Parents can't possibly know them all. Plus, if you only request specific assessments, those might be the only ones you get, and they may not be correct. Let the school personnel decide. Give them a chance to get it right. They are required to evaluate in every area of suspected disability. This is why you want to include as much as you can in your letter.

- Focus on observable behaviors: Mention things you or your child's teacher have observed, like difficulty staying focused, frustration with reading, or trouble with transitions.

- Optional medical diagnoses: If your child has a diagnosis (e.g., ADHD, dyslexia, anxiety), you can include it, but it's not required. Keep in mind that a medical diagnosis alone doesn't guarantee an IEP. However, it can be helpful in illustrating why you believe an evaluation is necessary.

Here's a sample letter to get you started:

Sample Letter:

Dear [Principal's Name or Teacher's Name],

I am formally requesting that my child, [Your Child's Full Name], who is in [Grade and Teacher's Name], be evaluated for special education services.

A few examples of why I believe this is necessary:

- It takes her two hours and significant parental assistance to complete her homework. She often says she doesn't understand the material.
- This summer, we noticed she struggled to read a menu at our favorite restaurant.
- She has difficulty following two-step instructions at home and in class.

Please send me a Permission to Evaluate form at your earliest convenience. If I do not hear back from you by [Insert Date, typically 10 days from the date you send the letter], I will follow up.

Sincerely,
[Your Full Name]

What Happens Next?

Once your request is received, the school has two options:

1. Agree to Evaluate: If it agrees, you'll receive a Permission to Evaluate (PTE) form. Read this carefully and sign it. The district then has 60 calendar days to complete the evaluation and hold a meeting to review the results. Some states use school days instead of calendar days, so be sure to check your state's regulations.

2. Refuse to Evaluate: If the school deny your request, it must provide you with a Prior Written Notice (PWN) explaining its decision.

Understanding Prior Written Notice (PWN)

PWN is one of your Procedural Safeguards under Individuals with Disabilities Education Act (IDEA). It's essentially the school's explanation for why it is refusing to evaluate or take another requested action. The notice should detail:

- What the school is proposing or refusing to do.
- The reasons for its decision.
- The data or information it used to make that decision.

Before signing anything, revisit the chapter on Procedural Safeguards in this book. Understanding your rights is critical at this stage. If you're unclear about any part of the PWN, ask questions. You're entitled to understand the decision before agreeing to it. I have more information about the PWN and its importance in a later chapter.

If the School Agrees to Evaluate

Once the school agrees to evaluate, the clock starts ticking. IDEA gives the district 60 calendar days (or a specific timeframe set by your state) to complete the evaluation and hold a meeting to review the results.

Use this time wisely. Dive into the rest of this book to familiarize yourself with the process and gather additional information about your child's needs. This is also an excellent time to begin organizing your IEP binder where you'll keep all correspondence, evaluations, and meeting notes.

Can't I Just Get My Child Evaluated Privately?

Sure you can. But per IDEA, the school only has to "consider" any information presented to it from an outside evaluator. It doesn't have to agree to the assessment or any of the strategies and accommodations listed by that evaluator. Most evaluations like this are educational and not medical. Insurance often does not cover this, so before you spend your money, ask the school to do it.

What Happens During the Evaluation?

The evaluation process involves a team of professionals assessing your child in areas of suspected disability. These assessments can cover:

- Academic skills (e.g., reading, math, writing).
- Cognitive abilities (e.g., problem solving, memory).
- Social-emotional development (e.g., relationships with peers, emotional regulation).
- Communication skills (e.g., speech, understanding language).
- Motor skills (e.g., fine and gross motor abilities).

Schools often use a mix of standardized tests, observations, and teacher/parent questionnaires to gather data.

Important: Ask for a list of the assessments they plan to use. While IDEA doesn't require schools to disclose every test upfront, many will share this information if you ask.

How Long Does It Take To Get an IEP?

It takes about one hundred days from start to finish, give or take a few days. It really does! From the Permission to Evaluate Form, to evaluations, IEP meetings and then implementation, it really can take that long. So, go with your gut. If you suspect a problem, don't delay.

Timelines vary by state, but here is a general guideline:

1. Parent sends email to the school with the request and waits for the school to respond. Some states specify that the school has five or 10 days to respond, but many do not. It can take 20–30 days, depending on holidays, snow days, etc.
2. The school sends the PTE Form to the parent, which they sign and return, usually 5–10 days.
3. The school then has 60 days to evaluate the child and write up the report.
4. If this is the first IEP for the child, the school then has 30 days to write up a proposed IEP.

The special education and IEP process is slow. As I said, you'll have to check your state's guidelines for specifics. This can be a very stressful time. But don't delay! You can see from above that, even if it's your intent to request evaluations on the first day of school, it could almost be Christmas until one is in place.

Common Challenges in the Process

These are the top three challenges in the process:

Delays: Unfortunately, delays happen. If the school misses the deadline for completing the evaluation, you can file a formal complaint with your state's Department of Education. Schools are legally bound to follow IDEA timelines.

Incomplete Assessments: If the evaluation doesn't address all areas of suspected disability, request additional assessments. For example, if your child struggles with sensory processing but the evaluation didn't include an OT assessment, ask for one.

Disagreement with Results: If you disagree with the evaluation findings, you have the right to request an Independent Educational Evaluation (IEE) at the school's expense. An IEE is conducted by a qualified professional who is not employed by the school district.

If the School Refuses to Evaluate

If the school denies your request for an evaluation, it must provide a PWN explaining their decision. Review this document carefully. Common reasons for denial include:

- The school believes your child's challenges can be addressed through general education interventions.
- It doesn't see evidence of a disability that affects educational performance.

If you disagree with the decision, you have options:

1. **Request Mediation:** Mediation is a voluntary process where a neutral third party helps resolve disputes between you and the school.
2. **File a State Complaint:** Contact your state's Department of Education to file a formal complaint.
3. **Request Due Process:** This is a more formal legal proceeding, similar to a court hearing. It's often a last resort but can be effective in resolving disputes.

A Word of Encouragement

If this feels overwhelming, take a deep breath. You've already taken an important step by recognizing your children's challenges and seeking help. That's no small feat, and it shows your dedication to their success.

Remember, the IEP process is a journey. There might be bumps along the way, but you're not alone. Use the resources in this book, connect with parent advocacy groups, and lean on your support network. You're doing an amazing job, and your children is lucky to have you in their corner.

With preparation, persistence, and the right resources, you'll navigate this process like a pro. Your children deserves the best, and you're the key to making that happen.

Your Play for This Chapter

1. Write and send your formal request for an evaluation if you need one. Use the sample letter as a guide.
2. If you don't need this information, share it with someone who does.
3. Follow up on your request to ensure it's being handled appropriately.

CHAPTER 6

Understanding IEP Eligibility

The two previous chapters explained that the Individualized Education Program (IEP) process starts with special education evaluations. And requesting all the evaluations you think your child needs should provide you with the necessary information for a solid IEP. Evaluations are the foundation of the entire IEP process. They're the blueprint, the guidebook, the *everything* when it comes to understanding your children's needs and getting them the support they require. Without solid evaluations, the rest of the IEP can quickly crumble like a badly built house.

What Happens During the Special Education Evaluation Process

You sent off a request to have your child evaluated. The school sent you a Permission to Evaluate (PTE) form (it's required by law!) and evaluated your child.

The next step is that an evaluation report is presented to the parent. Sometimes, this is sent via email before the eligibility meeting. Some schools choose to have the IEP eligibility meeting and the IEP meeting held back to back. Others hold them at separate times so the parent can digest all of the information. This is more common if it's the child's first ever evaluation or if the child has extensive needs.

Usually, subsequent evaluations and IEP meetings will always be held back to back.

What to Do When You Get the Evaluation Report

Here comes the moment of truth. You've got your child's IEP evaluation report, and now you're staring at pages of numbers, data, and terms you don't understand. Deep breaths.

Here's how to make sense of it:

1. Look at the Scores

   Pay attention to test results, but remember: *Scores aren't everything.* Just because your children has "average" scores doesn't mean they don't need help; many kids mask their struggles during tests.

2. Highlight the Discrepancies

   Compare the report findings to your own observations. If the report says your children has no behavioral issues, but you're getting daily phone calls from the school, well, something's off.

3. Ask Questions

   During the meeting, don't hesitate to ask for clarification. For example:

   - What do these scores mean in plain language?
   - How do these results impact their eligibility?
   - What supports will be put in place based on these findings?

Remember, the school is required to provide you with someone who can explain all of this to you in a manner in which you understand. Many parents do not ask for this because they do not want to appear like they don't know. But I remind all of my clients: This is the school psychologist's job. All day, every day, they are evaluating kids and creating these reports. Of course, this is easier for them! But, just like they could not walk into your workplace and instantly know how to do your job, you shouldn't expect yourself to do theirs.

What If You Disagree with the School's Special Education Evaluations?

Disagreement with an evaluation is common. Maybe the report doesn't align with what you see at home, or the recommendations fall short. Here's what to do:

Request an Independent Educational Evaluation (IEE)

If you disagree with the school's findings, you have the right to request an IEE at public expense. Send this request in writing and cite your disagreement with the school's evaluation. I cover IEEs in much more detail in Chapter 28. Asking for an IEE is not a move for novices because the school is required to file for Due Process if it refuses your request. Before requesting an IEE, it's essential you know all of your rights.

Understanding the Criteria and Categories

Determining eligibility for an Individualized Education Program (IEP) is one of the most critical steps in ensuring your child receives the support they need in school. But for many parents, this process can feel like deciphering a secret code. Words like "adverse impact" and "educational benefit" get thrown around, leaving you wondering if the school is deliberately trying to confuse you. (Spoiler: It might be.)

This chapter is your guide to understanding IEP eligibility, the disability categories under the Individuals with Disabilities Education Act (IDEA), and what to do if your child doesn't meet the criteria or if the school tells you they don't.

What Is IEP Eligibility?

To qualify for an IEP, a child must meet two criteria:

1. Have a qualifying disability under IDEA.
2. The disability must adversely affect the child's ability to access or progress in the general education curriculum, necessitating specialized instruction.

Let's break that down:

- A diagnosis alone (like ADHD or dyslexia) doesn't guarantee eligibility. The key is whether the disability affects the child's ability to learn and thrive in the classroom.
- The phrase "adversely affect" is a bit vague, which is why you'll often need strong documentation, evaluations, and a good dose of persistence.

The 13 Categories of Eligibility Under IDEA

The law outlines 13 categories of disabilities under which a child can qualify for an IEP. Understanding these categories is essential because they frame how your child's needs are assessed and supported.

1. **Autism (AU)**
   - This category includes a range of developmental disabilities, such as Autism Spectrum Disorder (ASD), which affects communication, behavior, and social interaction.
   - Signs might include difficulty with verbal and nonverbal communication, repetitive behaviors, or challenges in social situations.
   - Schools often require evaluations that include observations, developmental history, and autism-specific assessments.
2. **Deaf-Blindness**
   - This rare category applies to children with both hearing and visual impairments, creating severe communication and educational challenges.
   - Eligibility here focuses on whether the combined impairments prevent the child from accessing traditional educational supports provided to students with only hearing or vision loss.

3. Deafness
   - Children qualify under this category if they have a severe hearing impairment that affects their ability to process language, even with amplification devices.
   - While many children with hearing loss qualify under this category, some may instead fall under "Hearing Impairment" depending on the severity and impact.

4. Emotional Disturbance (ED)
   - This broad category includes conditions like anxiety, depression, bipolar disorder, or severe emotional dysregulation.
   - Signs include difficulty building or maintaining relationships, inappropriate behaviors, or an inability to learn that can't be explained by other factors.
   - Emotional Disturbance is often misunderstood. Many parents hear "behavior problem" instead of "mental health need," but the two aren't interchangeable.

5. Hearing Impairment (HI)
   - Unlike "Deafness," this category covers children with any degree of hearing loss that adversely affects educational performance.
   - Schools may provide accommodations, such as FM systems, speech therapy, or captioning services to address these needs.

6. Intellectual Disability (ID)
   - Formerly known as "mental retardation," this category refers to significant limitations in intellectual functioning and adaptive behaviors.
   - Children may struggle with problem solving, reasoning, or day-to-day life skills. Eligibility typically requires an IQ score below 70 and evaluations of adaptive functioning.

7. Multiple Disabilities (MD)
   - This category is for children who have two or more disabilities that create complex educational needs that can't be met by addressing only one condition.
   - For example, children with cerebral palsy and blindness may qualify under this category because their needs intersect.

8. Orthopedic Impairment (OI)
   - This category includes physical disabilities that limit a child's ability to move or navigate the school environment, such as cerebral palsy, spina bifida, or amputations.
   - Eligibility focuses on how the condition impacts the child's ability to participate in physical and educational activities.

9. Other Health Impairment (OHI)
   - Perhaps the broadest category, OHI covers conditions that limit a child's strength, energy, or alertness. Examples include ADHD, epilepsy, diabetes, or chronic illnesses like cystic fibrosis.

- ADHD is the most common condition under this category, and parents often face resistance when advocating for IEPs for children with ADHD. Documentation from healthcare providers is usually critical.

10. Specific Learning Disability (SLD)

    - This category covers difficulties with specific academic skills, such as reading (dyslexia), writing (dysgraphia), or math (dyscalculia).

    - SLD is the most common eligibility category in the United States, and schools often use data from classroom performance, evaluations, and Response to Intervention (RTI) programs to determine eligibility.

11. Speech or Language Impairment (SLI)

    - Children with speech or language impairments may have difficulty articulating sounds, understanding language, or using language to communicate.

    - Speech therapy is one of the most common services provided under this category.

12. Traumatic Brain Injury (TBI)

    - This category is for children with brain injuries caused by an external force (e.g., a car accident, fall, or sports injury) that affect learning, memory, or physical functioning.

    - While rare, children with TBI often require extensive accommodations and specialized supports.

13. Visual Impairment (VI), Including Blindness

    - This category covers children with partial sight or blindness that impacts their ability to learn.

    - Supports might include Braille instruction, orientation and mobility training, or assistive technology like screen readers.

Does It Really Matter Which Box Is Checked?

YES.

If you asked me this question just a few years ago, I'd say, "Nah, doesn't matter." I felt that as long as the child's needs were being met, all areas of need were identified, and each area of need was sufficiently addressed and supported, then this was a battle that parents didn't necessarily have to fight.

I feel differently now. Mind you, if your child's needs are otherwise being met, and you just don't have the time, energy, or cognitive horsepower to fight this battle, that's up to you. I will never be the advocate that tells parents they have to fight every battle. We all have our limits.

But think is my thinking now:

First and foremost, I want the child you see on paper to match the child that is sitting in front of me. If he has dyslexia (and we have that documented), I want it to say SLD, not OHI. If the child has autism, I want it to say autism, not ED.

You might think, "Well, if needs are otherwise being met, why?"

Well, first, I have found too many times that classification drives placement. It shouldn't but it does. If my child needs an autism support classroom, I want him there. Not a multiple disabilities or ED classroom and vice versa. The IEP eligibility category that your child gets is the team's high level view of how it sees your child. You want this to be accurate.

Also, if the school evaluations are pointing toward a different disability, then maybe the evaluation process needs to be looked at. Were the right evaluations done? Were all the areas of suspected need evaluated? Is it time to ask for an IEE?

The other reason is this: I have never once, in 15 years of attending IEP meetings for thousands of families, seen an IEP team get everything right except the disability eligibility category. Chances are, if this is incorrect, there are other flaws in the IEP. The eligibility category drives the "high level view" of the child. We want the child in front of us to match the child on paper.

The disability category, or "box" your children qualify under, doesn't dictate the specific services they receive. IDEA requires that IEPs be individualized based on your children's unique needs, not their diagnosis or eligibility category. For example, a child with ADHD might qualify under Other Health Impairment (OHI) in one district, while another child with the same condition might qualify under Specific Learning Disability (SLD). The key is that their needs—such as support with attention, executive functioning, or reading—are addressed in the IEP, no matter the category.

It can also matter, however, in situations where certain categories carry stigmas or assumptions that could unintentionally limit your child's opportunities. For instance:

- Children categorized under Emotional Disturbance (ED) may be unfairly viewed as "just a behavior problem," potentially overshadowing their academic needs.
- Children under Speech or Language Impairment (SLI) might be overlooked for academic support if the team assumes their challenges are limited to communication.

There are rare cases where the category can directly impact the type of supports your child is eligible for:

1. State-Specific Programs: Some state-funded programs or services may only be available to children under certain categories, like Autism (AU) or Deaf-Blindness.
2. Transition Planning: As your child ages, the eligibility category might influence access to specific vocational or adult-transition programs.

In these cases, it's worth having a conversation with the team to ensure your child's needs are being documented and addressed under the most appropriate category.

Ultimately, the category is a tool to open the door to services and not a definitive statement about your child. If the team insists on one category over another but your child's needs are being fully met, don't stress over the box. But if the box becomes a barrier to getting your children the support they need, it's worth pushing back and asking for clarification or reconsideration. Remember, the law is on your side, and your child's success is what truly matters.

What Happens If Your Child Doesn't Qualify?

Nothing feels more frustrating than knowing your children are struggling but being told they don't meet the criteria for an IEP. If this happens, don't give up. Here's what you can do:

1. Request a 504 Plan
   - If your children don't qualify for an IEP, they might be eligible for a 504 Plan under Section 504 of the Rehabilitation Act.
   - A 504 Plan provides accommodations (like extended time on tests or preferential seating) but doesn't include specialized instruction.
2. Dispute the Decision
   - If you disagree with the school's determination, you have the right to appeal. This might involve requesting an Independent Educational Evaluation (IEE) or filing a complaint.
   - Keep all communication in writing and document your concerns thoroughly.
3. Monitor and Reassess
   - Sometimes, a child's needs become clearer over time. You can request a re-evaluation if their situation changes or if new evidence emerges.
4. Seek Outside Support
   - Private tutoring, therapy, or educational advocacy can bridge the gap while you work with the school to secure services.

What Eligibility Really Means

Eligibility for an IEP is about more than checking boxes; it's about ensuring your children have the tools and support they need to succeed. Whether your children qualify under Autism, SLD, or OHI, the focus should always be on their unique needs, not just their diagnosis.

The end goal and indication of a solid IEP is that the child in front of us matches the child on paper. That starts with the appropriate eligibility category.

Advocating for evaluations (and beyond) isn't easy. It's exhausting, emotional, and, let's be honest, sometimes makes you want to scream into a pillow. But remember: Every piece of data, every email, and every meeting is part of building the foundation for your child's success.

IEP evaluations are the first step in understanding what your child truly needs to succeed. They provide the data and insights that guide every decision, goal, and support service in the IEP. They should be the baselines for your child's present levels section. When done well, evaluations empower you to advocate confidently and ensure the school team has a clear picture of your child's challenges and strengths.

The process isn't always easy, and it can feel overwhelming at times, but you're not alone in this. With the right tools, knowledge, and persistence, you can make sure your child has a meaningful and effective IEP. It all starts with solid evaluations, and you've got this.

Your Play for This Chapter

Your play for this chapter is to review your child's evaluation report(s) and determine if any areas of eligibility were missed. If so, ask for those specific evaluations.

PART 2

The IEP Starting Lineup

I thought about naming this part of the book something about either rookies or the practice squad. An NFL practice squad is a group of players who are signed to a team but not on the active roster. It practices, but it doesn't play unless it called up due to an injured player or something.

But neither of those names felt quite right. First of all, while some of you may be rookies in the sense that you don't have a lot of experience or knowledge, you may have been attending IEP meetings for years.

And, well, whether we like it or not, there is no practice squad in IEPs. From the get-go, every move you make counts. If we play this terribly, we won't ever get cut from this team or traded. We will just get worse and worse until we learn to play better.

Then it dawned on me: fundamentals. Just as athletes need to know the fundamentals of their sport, IEP parents need to know the fundamentals of IEPs. And that's what is in this section of the book.

IEPs are complex documents, but when you look at each component, it's much less scary or overwhelming. In fact, they even start to make sense! Over the next several chapters, I will explain the sections of an IEP, why they matter, and what to look for when troubleshooting or advocating.

PART 2

The IEP Starting Lineup

CHAPTER 7

The IEP Basics and the Cover Page

As we begin this walk through of an individualized education program (IEP) document, there are a few things to remember.

First, I will be providing snippets of examples of blank IEP documents from various states. The Individuals with Disabilities Education Act (IDEA) "leaves it up to the states" as far as how they will implement IDEA and provide special education. IDEA tells us the "what" but it does not tell us the "how." "How" it's done is left up to the states, which is why forms can vary.

There is not one required IEP form or document. As long as the IEP has all the required components, it can be on any piece of paper. You could even write it on notebook paper if you wanted.

As we go through the various parts of the IEP in Section 2 (Chapters 7–19) and I provide examples, remember that I am providing just that: examples. None of what I am showing is *required* per IDEA.

Many school districts subscribe to software platforms that build IEPs. This is important to know because over the years, I have heard from many parents they were told by their IEP team that a software program precluded them from doing something, usually in response to making a change to the IEP.

Parents have been told things like:

- IEP Present Levels can only be 200 words because our program does not allow more words than that.

- We cannot make that change to your IEP because the "IEP has been closed," and our software program does not allow changes after it has closed.

A software program's limitations do not supersede a child's nor a parent's rights in the IEP process. Even if it is not convenient for an IEP team to make changes, requesting changes is a parent's right.

IEP Cover Page Basics

For most people, the cover page may seem pretty benign. But you'd be surprised at how many issues arise from this page, which is shown in Figure 7.1.

The cover page should have the basic information about your child.

- Name, address, parents
- Grade, school
- IEP Dates

Schools write IEPs with parental input, but it will be a school staff person who does the physical act of writing the IEP. But parents can always request to have items added or omitted from any part of the IEP they do not feel is warranted, including the cover page.

A cover page seems simple, so where do the problems come up?

First, many IEP cover pages have a section that says "other" or "additional information" or "additional notes." For most students, it makes sense that this part should be blank. And here's why.

Mind you, this is a worst-case scenario, but it has happened to two of my clients. And that is, their IEP was left on top of a pile of papers on a teacher's desk. And, in that "other" section, the child's diagnoses were listed. Do not do this.

Side note: This was an egregious Family Educational Rights and Privacy Act (FERPA) violation. It's a federal law that protects the privacy of student education records and gives parents certain rights regarding their child's records.

In addition to having a child's protected information out where everyone could see, that information was just unnecessary on the cover page. IEPs are evaluation-driven or needs-driven (needs determined by evaluations), not diagnosis-driven. A diagnosis is not required to get an IEP, nor does it guarantee an IEP.

Many of our kids have very rare diagnoses. If I told you my son's condition, you'd probably never have heard of it. Most people have not. So, what use is it to put it on his IEP if no one knows what it is?

Third, even for the common diagnoses like autism or ADHD, it is not beneficial to put it on a cover page. Every child with ADHD or autism presents differently. Each of us comes to the table with preconceived biases when you say one of those words. We all have our own picture of what ADHD looks like, based on our own life experiences. What if that child presents very differently? The children's needs and all of their characteristics should be listed in Present Levels, which we'll get to in Chapter 11. But present levels are what describe the child, but there is too much information to be included on the cover pages.

Finally, many diagnoses carry incredible negative stigmas with them. This is what happened with both of my clients. Since the teachers left the IEPs out for all to see, other kids saw them and saw the diagnoses listed on the front page. These two students were bullied relentlessly for their entire school careers to the point of suicidal ideations.

I cannot describe the pain and suffering those families went through. I would never want to see it happen to another child, which is why I am such a firm proponent of "no information on the cover page."

INDIVIDUALIZED EDUCATION PROGRAM (IEP)
Student's Name:

INDIVIDUALIZED EDUCATION PROGRAM (IEP)   **School Age**

Student's Name:

IEP Team Meeting Date (mm/dd/yy):

IEP Implementation Date (Projected Date when Services and Programs Will Begin): _____

Anticipated Duration of Services and Programs: _____

Date of Birth: _____

Age: _____

Grade: _____

Anticipated Year of Graduation: _____

Local Education Agency (LEA): _____

County of Residence: _____

Name and Address of Parent/Guardian/Surrogate: _____   Phone (Home): _____

_____   Phone (Work): _____

_____

Other Information: _____

The LEA and parent have agreed to make the following changes to the IEP without convening an IEP meeting, as documented by:

Date of Revision(s)	Participants/Roles	IEP Section(s) Amended

February 1, 2020

FIGURE 7.1   IEP Cover Page Sample

IEP Start Dates

On the cover page, there should be a start day for the IEP. It's usually listed right on the front page. Other important dates should be listed there as well, such as graduation dates.

IEP students are entitled to a 13th, 14th, or even 15th year of school if their needs warrant it. Some may consider it predetermination by listing a graduation date on the cover page, but it can give you good insight as to what your IEP team is thinking or going to recommend.

I have come across many parents who are in a panic in April or May of their child's senior year, and they proclaim, "He's not ready to graduate!"

If plans have not been made for this 13th year or beyond, it's very difficult to right the ship during spring of the senior year. If you want your child to have those additional years for IEP transition (and we'll deal with the IEP transition section in a later chapter), you should start as soon as possible. But stating an anticipated graduation date on the cover page can be a starting point.

Family Information

You'll want to include the child's name, address, and contact information for whoever has legal custody of your child on the cover page. Your school is required to communicate with whoever has legal custody. Unfortunately, with the American divorce rate at around 40% today, this information is more important than you might think.

School personnel or IEP teams will not, and should not, get involved in family disputes like divorce and custody. If you have legal custody of the child or your residence is the child's primary residence, that is the address that should be on the IEP. If it is incorrect, you can provide proof and ask for a record change.

Divorce is stressful and expensive. Still, you may need to go back and get with your divorce attorney and get things clarified on paper. If your ex has put the new spouse or boyfriend/girlfriend name on the IEP and he or she does not have any form of legal custody, I would not ask to have it removed unless I can prove so by providing a custody agreement.

This follows through for all parts of the IEP, such as parental input, IEP meeting invitations, and so on. Your school is required to communicate with whomever has legal custody. Only ask them to do otherwise unless you have the documentation to back it up. I get it, really I do. If you and your ex have very different parenting styles and different expectations, an IEP can only make it worse. But a parent should not expect an IEP team to make decisions that should have been made during a divorce proceeding.

I've encountered this often as an advocate. Parents don't want a new spouse or girlfriend at the IEP meeting. If your ex has joint custody, then he or she is permitted to invite people to the IEP meeting. For years people have told me that I'm such a stickler for "getting everything written on the IEP." Yes, I am!

It saves so many headaches later when we all know what the expectations are. The same should go for your divorce and custody arrangement. You want it clearly spelled out who has education decision-making authority. There's also the situation where the parents never married. They had kids, but then the relationship just dissolved and they went their separate ways. Since there was no marriage, there's no need for a divorce, right?

I recommend that you speak with a family attorney about this and custody arrangements in these situations. The IEP team will not and should not get involved in family disputes like this, so make sure your educational rights are clearly defined in your divorce decree.

I have seen situations where the custody arrangements and the IEP were both contentious. Some IEP teams will side with the parent with whom they agree already, and it can get very ugly quickly. Try to get on the same page with your ex about your IEP children and what you envision for them for the future.

Regardless of what happened in your relationship, inside the IEP meeting you need to be a united front.

LEA Contact Information

Also on the cover page is the Local Education Agency (LEA) information, otherwise known as your school district. I don't know why it doesn't just say "school district," but that's how the government likes to word things sometimes.

The LEA is responsible for implementation of the IEP. This section should list a representative person who will be your contact person if you wish to request an IEP meeting or further evaluations or use your dispute resolution options.

This might seem to be obvious information, but it does confuse parents at times when they see an unfamiliar face at IEP meetings or an unfamiliar name on the documents. A parent does not get to choose who is the LEA; the school district chooses. The LEA is the steward of the school district's resources, which is important to remember.

I wish these situations were not as adversarial as they are, but they are. The LEA is there to represent the district, not your child. You are there to represent your child.

Your Play for This Chapter

Look at your child's IEP cover sheet for any of the above listed items.

CHAPTER 8

The Signature Page and IEP Team

It might seem excessive to dedicate an entire chapter to the individualized education program (IEP) signature page, but this often-overlooked piece of paper has more significance than meets the eye. The signature page isn't just about who attended the meeting; it can reveal a lot about the process and offer insights into potential challenges or opportunities for advocacy.

In most IEPs, the IEP signature page is the second page of the IEP. During a meeting, it might be pulled out so that everyone can sign it. Let's break down why this page matters, common issues to watch for, and how you can leverage it to improve your child's IEP process.

The Basics of the IEP Signature Page

The signature page is where all team members present at the meeting record their attendance. It typically includes:

- Each participant's name and role, e.g., special education teacher, general education teacher, Local Education Agency (LEA) representative
- A signature line to confirm their presence

This page plays a critical role in documenting the process and ensuring that the required team members participated.

IDEA Requirements for IEP Team Members

The Individuals with Disabilities Education Act (IDEA) specifies who must be part of an IEP team:

- Parents of the child
- At least one general education teacher (if the child is or may be participating in general education)

- At least one special education teacher or service provider
- A representative of the LEA who:
  - Is qualified to supervise specially designed instruction.
  - Knows the general education curriculum.
  - Has the authority to allocate resources. (This person cannot say, "I don't have the authority to approve that request.")
- Someone who can interpret the instructional implications of evaluation results
- At the discretion of the parent or district, other individuals with expertise or knowledge about the child
- When appropriate, the child with a disability

The following sections go into more details about the people at the meeting

Related Service Providers

While related service providers like occupational therapists (OTs) or speech-language pathologists (SLPs) often play a vital role in your child's education, they are not required members of the IEP team under IDEA. Of course, it is best practice to include them in a meeting, but in today's IEP world, their caseloads often prevent this. This is one of those times that parents have to pick their battles as far as pushing for the person to be there.

This doesn't mean their input is unimportant: far from it!

- If a related service provider cannot attend the meeting, the school must provide the provider's input in writing.
- If written input isn't sufficient, you can request a separate meeting with that provider to discuss their recommendations.

General and Special Education Teachers

The law states that one general education and one special education teacher must attend, but it doesn't specify that it must be your child's specific teacher. This becomes an issue during the summer when teachers may be on vacation or during extended leaves like maternity leave. While having your child's actual teacher is ideal, the school can send another teacher from the same grade or subject.

If this meeting is during the summer and you're trying to fine tune some items on your IEP for fall, maybe your child's specific teacher has not even been assigned yet. On the other hand, if there are significant issues and it's during the school year, you can ask to reschedule the meeting when your child's teacher(s) can be there. One parental right in IDEA is meaningful parent participation in the IEP process, and if having the correct staff people there is essential to this right, speak up.

Someone to Explain Evaluations

This is a big one. IDEA requires that someone at the meeting be able to explain your child's evaluations and their instructional implications. Don't hesitate to ask questions if you don't understand the results. Evaluations are often filled with jargon, and it's the school's responsibility to ensure you understand what they mean for your child's education.

I know what it's like to feel intimidated at IEP meetings, and asking for help may make you feel even more vulnerable. But let me ask you this: What do you do for a living? Do you think that if your child's teachers went to your workplace, that they'd instantly know how to do everything at your job? Probably not!

So, why are you holding yourself to this standard? Of course you don't know how to interpret education evaluations. None of us does unless we do it for a living. This is one of those tough love moments where I tell you that you've got to step out of your comfort zone and ask for help. It's essential that you understand your child's data, or you'll never know if your child is making progress or not.

A Few Other Notes About Your IEP Team

In most situations, your child may have a related service provider (PT, OT, et al.) or a resource room teacher for more than one year. Other than that, most of your child's teachers may change every year.

I say this because I get many questions from parents about keeping certain team members because it's going so well for your child or about removing people from the IEP team because their presence in meetings is adversarial. Or even obnoxious sometimes!

I can say this with a lot of experience. I know the heartbreak of watching your child's progress come to a screeching halt because a provider changed. And I've sat in a lot of IEP meetings with personnel who were rude. I've had teachers or providers who just did not connect with my kid or a client's child.

Your school is bound to the IEP. They are required to provide everything that's in it. That does not mean a specific person needs to do it. And it is not a reasonable expectation to have a specific person named in your IEP because that person could resign tomorrow and leave the school out of compliance. The school is required to provide the services in the IEP. Keep that as your target in advocacy.

Do your children have a setback every time their aide changes? Document that and advocate from that angle rather than asking for a specific person.

As far as requesting that a specific person not attend your IEP meetings, I don't think I have ever done this as a parent or for a client. Because the simple answer is it's not the battle I choose to fight. I don't make it a practice to fight battles that I can't win, and this is a very difficult battle to win.

If someone on your team is adversely affecting your meetings, figure out a way to rise above it. Because the school can invite any staff it chooses as long as it meets the "has knowledge of the child" component. And now you've let them know they got under your skin. Don't let one player throw off your whole game; stay focused, adjust your strategy, and play to win.

Signing the Signature Page

The signature page is one of the most misunderstood parts of the IEP. Let's clarify a few common misconceptions:

What Does Your Signature Mean?

Signing the signature page does not mean you agree with the IEP. It simply acknowledges that you attended the meeting. You do not have to agree to the IEP that day at the IEP meeting. Take your time and read all of it thoroughly and then get back to the team. This ensures that you have time to review all sections of the IEP thoroughly.

When Does Your Signature Matter?

A parent's signature is required to initiate services for a child's first IEP. However, in most states, a parent's signature is not required for subsequent IEPs. Only four states—California, Massachusetts, Montana, and Virginia—require parental signatures for every IEP.

What If You Refuse to Sign?

In most states, refusing to sign the IEP or attendance sheet doesn't stop the process. While withholding your signature might feel like reclaiming power, it's a mostly symbolic gesture and can signal to the team that you don't fully understand your rights.

Leveraging the Signature Page

The signature page isn't just a formality: It can be a powerful tool in the IEP process. For one, it can address what I call the "musical chairs IEP meeting" or revolving door of staff coming and going and interrupting the meeting.

A common parent frustration is when team members come and go during the meeting. This can feel chaotic and disrespectful, especially when you've taken time off work to attend.

Here's how to handle it:

- **Control the Signature Page**: When the signature page comes to you, keep it near you. As team members leave or arrive, jot down the times next to their names. This creates a clear record of who was present for what portions of the meeting.
- **Pause the Meeting**: If someone enters or leaves while someone else is speaking, politely pause the discussion. For example, say, "Let's take a moment to let Mr. Smith get settled so he can hear what we're discussing."

These small actions can discourage the revolving door dynamic and ensure the meeting stays focused.

A Note on Gifted Students

If your child is gifted or twice-exceptional (gifted with a learning disability), be aware that not all states provide services for gifted students under IDEA. For example, in Pennsylvania, gifted students are served through a Gifted IEP (GIEP), and a Teacher of the Gifted must be included on the IEP team. Check your state's regulations to understand how this applies to your situation.

The signature page may seem like a small detail, but it serves an important purpose in documenting the IEP process and ensuring required team members are present. Use it to your advantage by keeping track of attendance, identifying gaps in participation, and holding the team accountable.

By understanding the nuances of the signature page, you can strengthen your role as an advocate and ensure your child's needs are front and center.

Your Play for This Chapter

Review your child's IEP signature page. Are all required team members listed? Did they attend the meeting, or was their input provided in another form? Take notes and address any concerns at your next meeting.

CHAPTER 9

Procedural Safeguards and Medicaid

At first glance, the Procedural Safeguards and Medicaid signature page (see Figure 9.1) might seem like just another formality, but it's actually a critical part of the individualized education program (IEP) process. While it might feel like a quick "sign here" moment, this page carries significant weight in protecting your rights as a parent and ensuring that the resources your child needs are accessible.

This chapter will cover the two parts of this page: Procedural Safeguards and Medicaid. We'll unpack why these forms matter, common pitfalls to avoid, and how you can use them to advocate effectively for your child.

Procedural Safeguards

Let's talk about the Procedural Safeguards section first (see Figure 9.1).

What Are Procedural Safeguards?

Procedural Safeguards are essentially your "parents' rights" in the IEP process. They outline your rights under the Individuals with Disabilities Education Act (IDEA), including:

- Your right to participate in the IEP process
- Your right to dispute decisions through due process, mediation, or a state complaint
- Your child's rights, including protections during disciplinary actions

The Procedural Safeguards booklet is a legal requirement, and schools must provide it to you at least once per school year. By signing the accompanying page, you acknowledge that you've received this document.

INDIVIDUALIZED EDUCATION PROGRAM (IEP)
Student's Name:

PROCEDURAL SAFEGUARDS NOTICE

I have received a copy of the *Procedural Safeguards Notice* during this school year. The *Procedural Safeguards Notice* provides information about my rights, including the process for disagreeing with the IEP. The school has informed me whom I may contact if I need more information.

Signature of Parent/Guardian/Surrogate: _____

MEDICAL ASSISTANCE PROGRAM BILLING NOTICE

(Applicable only to parents who have consented to the release of billing information to Medical Assistance programs)

I understand that the school may charge the School-Based Access Program ("SBAP")—or any program that replaces or supplements the SBAP—the cost of certain special education and related services described in my child's IEP. To make these charges to the SBAP, the school will release to the administrator of that program the name, age, and address of my child, verification of Medicaid eligibility for my child, a copy of my child's IEP, a description of the services provided and the times and dates during which such services were provided to my child, and the identity of the provider of such services. *I understand that such information will not be disclosed, and such charges will not be made, unless I consent to the disclosure.* I acknowledge that I have provided written consent to disclose such information.

I understand that my consent is ongoing from year-to-year unless and until I withdraw it. I can withdraw my consent in writing, or orally if I am unable to write, at any time. My refusal to consent or my withdrawal of consent will not relieve the school of the obligation to provide, at no cost to me or my family, any service or program to which my child is entitled under the Individuals with Disabilities Education Act ("IDEA") or that is necessary to enable my child to receive a free appropriate public education as described in my child's IEP.

I understand that the school cannot—

Require me or my family to sign up for or enroll in any public benefits or insurance program, such as Medicaid, as a condition of receiving a free appropriate public education for my child;

Require me or my family to incur any expense for the provision of a free appropriate public education to my child, including co-payments and deductibles, unless it agrees to pay such expenses on my or my family's behalf;

Cause a decrease in available lifetime coverage or any other insured benefit;

Cause me or my family to pay for services that would otherwise be covered by a public benefits or insurance program and that are required for my child outside the time that he or she is in school;

Risk the loss of eligibility for home and community-based waivers, based on aggregate health-related expenditures.

FIGURE 9.1   Procedural Safeguards and Medicaid page

Why Are Procedural Safeguards Important?

While the booklet itself may be dry, tedious, and written in dense legal language, it is the cornerstone of your advocacy. It explains:

- How to challenge decisions you don't agree with
- What to do if your child is suspended or facing disciplinary action
- How to access Independent Education Evaluation (IEEs) and other resources

These rights are especially crucial if the IEP process becomes contentious. Unfortunately, I've seen many parents struggle in disputes because they didn't understand their rights or had never read the booklet.

Common Issues with Procedural Safeguards

The following are three common issues with the Procedural Safeguards:

1. Language Barriers:

   Schools are required to provide the booklet in a language you can understand. Most state Departments of Education offer these documents in multiple languages. If you need a translated version, ask the school.
2. Incomplete Booklets:

   I've encountered parents with booklets missing entire sections or pages, often blamed on "copying errors." For example:
   - Missing even-numbered pages.
   - No list of resources or advocacy organizations in the back.

   Always check that your copy is complete. If you're unsure, compare it to an online version available from your state's Department of Education.

3. Failure to Read It:

   Let's face it: Reading a booklet that's 50+ pages of legalese isn't anyone's idea of a good time. But you don't have to read it all at once. Break it into manageable chunks and read it during downtime, such as while waiting at appointments or during soccer practice.

Why You Should Read Procedural Safeguards Before You Need Them

When your child is facing suspension, expulsion, or other significant challenges, it's a stressful time. That's not when you want to learn your rights for the first time.

For example:

- Discipline: Did you know that disciplining students with IEPs follows different rules than disciplining non-disabled peers?
- IEEs: If you disagree with the school's evaluation, you have the right to request an IEE at public expense.

Understanding these rights before you're in crisis can make a huge difference in how you handle the situation.

Secret Tip: This tip isn't a secret. Well, it is, but it shouldn't be. But you are entitled, as an IEP parent, to have your parental rights or the procedural safeguards explained to you! Remember when I told you to ask for help if you don't understand your child's evaluations because the school is required to provide you with someone? The same holds true here, too.

Bonus Pro Tip: If you're feeling spicy, your meetings have been adversarial recently, and you feel like your IEP rights are being trampled on, ask for this during the meeting. When they slide that little booklet across the table, just pause and say, "You know what, it's my right to have these explained to me, and I would like to do that now. There must be something I'm missing since our recent meetings are not going well."

If you want to see a room get quiet, this is the way to do it! While I have only done this twice in my entire career with clients, both times it did turn the mood of the meeting around.

I thought long and hard about how much I was going to include about Procedural Safeguards because I really, really, REALLY want you to read them. But then I thought some more, and hey, you're here now in this book reading. So, I'm going to share a few important things about your parents' rights and hopefully it will be interesting enough to make you want to read more.

Here are some highlights:

1. Right to Written Notice: Before the school does *anything* significant—evaluations, changes to services, or placement—it must give you prior written notice. This isn't optional, and it's your chance to understand (and potentially challenge) the school's decisions. I explain this more in a future chapter.

2. Dispute Resolution Options: When disagreements arise (and they will), safeguards ensure you have options, such as mediation, due process hearings, and even state complaints. Knowing these processes can level the playing field when the team isn't hearing you.

3. Parental Participation: This is your golden ticket. The law requires that parents are part of the IEP team. If you feel like a rubber stamp instead of a team member, this safeguard backs you up.

Bottom line: These are the rights that you have as an IEP parent, guaranteed by the federal government. The school is not going to beg you to learn and exercise your rights. Take ownership of this.

Medicaid

Now let's talk about the Medicaid section.

What Is the Medicaid Form About?

If your state participates in Medicaid expansion for children with disabilities, this form allows the school to bill Medicaid for services provided through your child's IEP, such as:

- Occupational therapy (OT)
- Physical therapy (PT)
- Speech therapy

Each state's Medicaid program operates differently, so it's important to understand how yours works.

Why Signing Matters

In many states, signing the Medicaid form helps schools access additional funding streams to support special education services. However, there are some nuances to be aware of:

1. Insurance Limits:

   If your private insurance covers therapy, Medicaid billing might count against your total number of allowed visits. For example:
   - Your child's insurance allows 30 OT visits per year.
   - The school provides OT through Medicaid.
   - If Medicaid counts those visits toward your limit, you might hit your cap faster than expected.

   Double-check with your insurance provider and state Medicaid rules to avoid financial surprises.

2. No Penalty for Refusal:

   Schools cannot withhold services if you refuse to sign the Medicaid form. IDEA guarantees that your child will receive the services outlined in their IEP, regardless of Medicaid billing.

3. Impact on Supplemental Services:

   In some states, signing the Medicaid form has no impact on your child's access to private therapy or services. Instead, it simply helps the school recover costs.

   If you're unsure about your state's Medicaid policies, consult a local parent advocacy group or your state's Department of Education for guidance.

Practical Tips for Handling These Forms

Here are some practical tips for handling both of these forms.

1. **Ask Questions:**

   Before signing the Medicaid form, ask your school about:
   - How Medicaid billing works in your state
   - Whether it will affect your private insurance or out-of-pocket costs

2. **Review Procedural Safeguards Annually:**

   Even if you've read the booklet before, it's worth revisiting each year. Laws and policies can change, and staying informed is key to effective advocacy.

3. **Verify Your Copy:**

   Check the booklet you're given for completeness. If any pages are missing or you suspect an error, request a new copy or access the digital version online.

The Procedural Safeguards and Medicaid signature page may seem like a small piece of the larger IEP puzzle, but it holds significant importance. It represents your rights, your child's protections, and the resources available to ensure their educational success.

By taking these steps, you're equipping yourself with the knowledge to navigate the IEP process confidently and effectively.

Now that we've covered these essential forms, let's move on to something even more critical: Special Factors. This is where the real fun begins!

Your Play for This Chapter

1. Get a copy of your state's Procedural Safeguards booklet and make a plan to read it. I say make a plan because it cannot be read in one sitting. Put it in your car and read it while waiting at sports practices: That's what I do! I still review mine at least once a year.

2. Research your state's Medicaid policies regarding children with disabilities.

3. Don't be afraid to ask questions or seek clarification about any forms you're asked to sign.

CHAPTER 10

Special Factors

The previous three chapters of this book might have opened your eyes to how even seemingly minor sections of the individualized education program (IEP) can have a significant impact. Now we're diving into a critical section: Special Factors (see Figure 10.1). This is where the IEP team considers specific challenges that could influence your child's ability to learn, participate, and succeed in school.

While the term "Special Factors" might sound abstract, its implications are very concrete. The Individuals with Disabilities Education Act (IDEA) mandates these considerations because they directly impact the effectiveness of the IEP. Yet disagreements over these checkboxes are common and often the starting point for many contentious IEP discussions.

What Are Special Factors?

Under IDEA, the IEP team is required to consider five "special factors" before developing the IEP. These are outlined in federal law, and here's what they entail:

1. Behavior: If children's behavior impedes their learning or the learning of others, the team must consider positive behavior interventions and supports.
2. Limited English Proficiency (LEP): If the children are an English language learner (ELL), their language needs must be addressed.
3. Visual Impairments: If the child is blind or visually impaired, the IEP must address the need for Braille instruction unless an evaluation shows it's unnecessary.
4. Communication Needs: For children who are deaf or hard of hearing, the IEP must consider their communication needs, including opportunities for direct communication in their language or mode of communication.
5. Assistive Technology (AT): The team must determine whether the children require assistive technology devices or services to support their learning.

While these factors might seem straightforward, the real challenge lies in interpretation. Parents and schools often disagree about whether a particular box should be checked "yes" or "no."

INDIVIDUALIZED EDUCATION PROGRAM (IEP)

Student's Name:

I. SPECIAL CONSIDERATIONS THE IEP TEAM MUST CONSIDER BEFORE DEVELOPING THE IEP. ANY FACTORS CHECKED AS "YES" MUST BE ADDRESSED IN THE IEP.

Is the student blind or visually impaired?

☐ Yes   The IEP must include a description of the instruction in Braille and the use of Braille unless the IEP team determines, after an evaluation of the student's reading and writing skills, needs, and appropriate reading and writing media (including an evaluation of the student's future needs for instruction in Braille or the use of Braille), that instruction in Braille or the use of Braille is not appropriate for the student.

☐ No

Is the student deaf or hard of hearing?

☐ Yes   The IEP must include a communication plan to address the following: language and communication needs; opportunities for direct communications with peers and professional personnel in the student's language and communication mode; academic level; full range of needs, including opportunities for direct instruction in the student's language and communication mode; and assistive technology devices and services. Indicate in which section of the IEP these considerations are addressed. The Communication Plan must be completed and is available at www.pattan.net

☐ No

Does the student have communication needs?

☐ Yes   Student needs must be addressed in the IEP (i.e., present levels, specially designed instruction (SDI), annual goals, etc.)

☐ No

Does the student need assistive technology devices and/or services?

☐ Yes   Student needs must be addressed in the IEP (i.e., present levels, specially designed instruction, annual goals, etc.)

☐ No

Does the student have limited English proficiency?

☐ Yes   The IEP team must address the student's language needs and how those needs relate to the IEP.

☐ No

FIGURE 10.1   Examples of the Special Factors section of an IEP

INDIVIDUALIZED EDUCATION PROGRAM (IEP)
Student's Name:

Does the student exhibit behaviors that impede his/her learning or that of others?

☐ Yes   The IEP team must develop a Positive Behavior Support Plan that is based on a functional assessment of behavior and that utilizes positive behavior techniques. Results of the functional assessment of behavior may be listed in the Present Levels section of the IEP with a clear measurable plan to address the behavior in the Goals and Specially Designed Instruction sections of the IEP or in the Positive Behavior Support Plan if this is a separate document that is attached to the IEP. A Positive Behavior Support Plan and a Functional Behavioral Assessment form are available at www.pattan.net

☐ No

Other (specify):

II. PRESENT LEVELS OF ACADEMIC ACHIEVEMENT AND FUNCTIONAL PERFORMANCE

Include the following information related to the student:

- Present levels of academic achievement (e.g., most recent evaluation of the student, results of formative assessments, curriculum-based assessments, transition assessments, progress toward current goals)
- Present levels of functional performance (e.g., results from a functional behavioral assessment, results of ecological assessments, progress toward current goals)
- Present levels related to current postsecondary transition goals if the student's age is 14 or younger if determined appropriate by the IEP team (e.g., results of formative assessments, curriculum-based assessments, progress toward current goals)
- Parental concerns for enhancing the education of the student
- How the student's disability affects involvement and progress in the general education curriculum
- Strengths
- Academic, developmental, and functional needs related to student's disability

III. TRANSITION SERVICES – This is required for students age 14 or younger if determined appropriate by the IEP team. If the student does not attend the IEP meeting, the school must take other steps to ensure that the student's preferences and interests are considered. Transition services are a coordinated set of activities for a student with a disability that is designed to be within a results oriented process, that is focused on improving the academic and functional achievement of the student with a disability to facilitate the student's movement from school to post school activities, including postsecondary education, vocational education, integrated employment (including supported employment), continuing and adult education, adult services, independent living, or community participation that is based on the individual student's needs taking into account the student's strengths, preferences, and interests.

February 1, 2020

FIGURE 10.1 *(Continued)*

Why Special Factors Matter

The checkboxes on this page guide the rest of the IEP process. A "yes" answer means the team must address that factor somewhere in the IEP. For example:

- A child who needs assistive technology will have that need outlined in their Present Levels, Goals, or Specially Designed Instruction (SDI).
- A student with behavior challenges may require a Functional Behavior Assessment (FBA) and a Behavior Intervention Plan (BIP).
- For Blind or Deaf students, if this box is checked, it triggers another set of requirements that schools must follow.

If a box is checked "no" when it should be "yes," it creates a significant gap in the IEP and can lead to unmet needs.

Common Pitfalls

Remember, IEPs follow a sequential process. As you go through the steps, if the information is incorrect, it will affect the integrity of the entire IEP going forward. What might seem like "just a checkbox" could have significant consequences.

Mislabeling Behavior

The behavior checkbox is one of the most misunderstood and misapplied areas. Schools often recognize disruptive behaviors but overlook quieter ones.

- Obvious behaviors: Aggression, yelling, or refusing to follow instructions are easy to spot.
- Subtle behaviors: Anxiety-related behaviors like task avoidance, excessive trips to the nurse, or school refusal often go unaddressed.

Behavior doesn't have to disrupt the entire class to impede learning. If your children are falling behind because of their behaviors—whether loud or quiet—this factor should be marked "yes."

Misinterpreting Assistive Technology

AT is another area where misunderstandings arise. Many teams hesitate to check "yes" because they assume it requires adding an AT-specific goal to the IEP. This is incorrect.

- Not all AT requires a goal. For example, a student might use a large-screen laptop, speech-to-text software, or noise-canceling headphones as accommodations. These do not need standalone goals but should still be documented in the IEP.

- Conversely, if the child needs to learn how to use a device effectively (e.g., learning to navigate a screen reader), that might warrant a goal.

Limited English Proficiency (LEP) Missteps

For bilingual students, distinguishing between learning disabilities and language barriers is crucial.

- Some schools incorrectly assume that all academic struggles are due to language issues and place students in English as a Second Language (ESL) programs instead of addressing underlying disabilities.
- Others assume bilingual students can't have disabilities. In reality, a child can be fluent in English and still have dyslexia, ADHD, or another learning challenge.

If your child is bilingual and struggling academically, push the team to conduct appropriate evaluations to determine whether a disability is present.

Skipping Communication Needs

For children who are deaf or hard of hearing, the communication checkbox, or the specific check boxes related to vision and hearing, ensure that their unique needs are addressed. Unfortunately, this factor is often treated as an afterthought.

- Does your child have opportunities to interact directly with peers and staff in their preferred communication mode (e.g., American Sign Language)?
- Are accommodations like interpreters, captioning, or communication devices provided consistently?

How to Advocate for Accurate Special Factors

Even if the team agrees to address the special factor later in the IEP, I recommend that parents advocate here. If the team is going to provide it, why not check the box?

1. Prepare in Advance: Before the IEP meeting, review this section and make a preliminary determination of which boxes should be checked "yes." Gather any supporting documentation, such as evaluation results or reports from therapists.
2. Ask Questions: If the team members checks "no" on a box you believe should be "yes," ask why. Request data or examples to support their decision.
3. Document Everything: If there's a disagreement, make sure your position is noted in the meeting minutes or follow up with an email summarizing your concerns.
4. Bring in Experts: If the team lacks the expertise to evaluate a specific need (e.g., AT or behavior), request an outside evaluation.

Special Focus on Behavior

The behavior factor deserves extra attention because it's often at the heart of many IEP disputes.

Addressing Behavior in the IEP

When the behavior box is checked "yes," the team must develop a Positive Behavior Support Plan (PBSP) or BIP. This plan should:

- Be based on a Functional Behavior Assessment (FBA)
- Use positive reinforcement rather than punitive measures
- Include measurable goals for improving behavior.

Special Factors as a Foundation

Remember, the Special Factors section is just the starting point. Once these checkboxes are completed, they guide the rest of the IEP. Here's how:

- If a children need AT, their Present Levels should describe how it's used, and their SDI should include it as an accommodation.
- If children have behavior challenges, their Goals should focus on building replacement behaviors or improving emotional regulation.

Each "yes" checkbox must connect to a specific part of the IEP.

The Special Factors page might seem like a small part of the IEP, but it has a ripple effect on every other section. By advocating for accurate and thoughtful consideration of these factors, you're laying the groundwork for a stronger, more effective IEP.

Your Play for This Chapter

1. Review Your Child's Special Factors Section: Look at each checkbox and ask yourself whether it accurately reflects your child's needs.
2. Prepare to Advocate: If you believe a box should be checked "yes" but the team disagrees, gather data and examples to support your case.
3. Follow Through: Ensure that any "yes" answers are addressed in the appropriate sections of the IEP.

CHAPTER 11

Present Levels

This chapter is one of my favorites, hands down. I could talk about Present Levels all day long. Why? Because individualized education program (IEP) Present Levels are everything. If you've ever wondered what makes or breaks an IEP, look no further. In my online training program, we dedicate more than two hours just to Present Levels. That's how crucial they are.

Let's get into the nitty-gritty of why Present Levels are the bedrock of an effective IEP and what you, as a parent, need to know to ensure this section is airtight.

Why Are IEP Present Levels So Important?

Present Levels of Performance (often called PLOP, PLAAFP, or PLAAPF, depending on your district's acronym-of-the-day obsession) are your children's "You Are Here" marker on the map of their educational journey. They paint a picture of where your child is right now: academically, socially, emotionally, and functionally.

Think of it like this: If the IEP is a house, Present Levels are the foundation. You wouldn't build a house on quicksand, right? If the foundation is shaky—if Present Levels are vague, incomplete, or just plain inaccurate—then everything else built on top of it (goals, services, accommodations, placement) will be a mess.

If your child's Present Levels aren't thorough, accurate, and specific, the entire IEP falls apart. A weak PLOP leads to goals that are too easy or difficult, services that don't address actual needs, and accommodations that miss the mark.

What Should a Strong IEP Present Levels Section Include?

A well-written Present Levels section provides an objective, data-driven, and detailed snapshot of your child. Here's what you should look for:

- **Academic Skills:** This includes specific details like reading levels (e.g., "reading at a third-grade level with 80% accuracy"), math competencies, and progress in other core subjects.

- **Functional Skills:** These cover daily living skills, organization, time management, and self-advocacy.
- **Social and Emotional Development:** How do your children interact with peers and adults? Can they regulate emotions effectively?
- **Behavior:** If behavior is a concern, this section should outline challenges, triggers, and successful interventions.
- **Strengths:** This isn't just fluff! Identifying your child's strengths (academic or personal) is essential for a well-rounded picture.
- **Parent Input:** Your observations are critical and should absolutely be included.

Sources of Data for Present Levels

So, where does all this information come from? Ideally, it's a combination of multiple sources:

- **Formal Evaluations and Assessments:** These provide objective, measurable data and form the backbone of Present Levels.
- **Teacher and Service Provider Input:** Anecdotes and observations from the classroom or therapy sessions can add depth.
- **Parent Input:** Your firsthand knowledge of your child's abilities and challenges at home is invaluable.
- **Report Cards and Work Samples:** These show trends over time and help create a fuller picture of your child's progress (or lack thereof).
- **Independent Evaluations:** If you've had private testing done, this is an important piece of the puzzle.

While anecdotes can be helpful, they should always be relevant and contextual. For instance, a single behavioral outburst from six months ago shouldn't dominate the narrative unless it reflects an ongoing pattern.

Common Mistakes to Watch For

Schools sometimes write Present Levels in ways that are vague, overly positive, or completely devoid of meaningful data. Here are some red flags to watch for:

- **Vague Statements:** "Alex is doing well in reading." What does "well" mean? Is Alex reading at grade level? How many words per minute? Always push for specifics.
- **Lack of Data:** Statements like "struggling with math" are meaningless without numbers or examples. Ask for test scores, work samples, or other measurable evidence.
- **Generic Language:** Phrases like "a joy to have in class" are nice but unhelpful unless tied to specific, measurable skills.
- **No Baseline Information:** Goals are built on Present Levels, so there must be a clear starting point. Without one, you can't measure progress.

How to Advocate for Strong Present Levels

If you feel that the Present Levels section doesn't accurately reflect your child, you absolutely have the right to challenge it. Here's how:

1. **Request Data:** Everything in the IEP should be backed by evidence. If the school says your children are improving in emotional regulation, ask for specifics: How often are they self-regulating now compared to before? Is there a measurable decrease in meltdowns?
2. **Submit Parent Input in Writing:** Your observations matter. Share what you're seeing at home, whether it's challenges with homework, social struggles, or successes in certain areas.
3. **Call Out Inaccuracies:** If the Present Levels section glosses over significant challenges or paints an overly rosy picture, speak up. Be polite but firm, and always follow up in writing.
4. **Push for Specificity:** Don't settle for vague or generic language. Specifics are critical for crafting effective goals and services.

A Real-Life Example

Let's say the Present Levels section says "Sam struggles with math." Not good enough, right? A better version would be:

> *"Sam is currently able to solve single-digit addition and subtraction problems independently but requires teacher assistance for multi-step word problems. Recent assessments show Sam completes four out of 10 multi-step problems correctly with assistance, compared to two out of 10 at the start of the school year."*

See the difference? The second version provides a clear starting point and shows measurable progress.

The Present Levels section isn't just a formality. It's the foundation for your child's entire educational plan. If it's not accurate or detailed, the rest of the IEP will be off. And if the school paints an overly positive picture, your child could even lose eligibility for certain services.

As a parent, your role is to ensure that your child's Present Levels are as thorough, accurate, and specific as possible. This is where you lay the groundwork for effective goals, services, and accommodations.

Additional Tips for Improving Present Levels

Here are additional tips for improving Present Levels:

- **Use Current Data:** Make sure the data are up-to-date. Information from years ago isn't useful for today's IEP.

- **Highlight Progress and Challenges:** A good Present Levels section acknowledges both strengths and areas of need.
- **Advocate for Comprehensive Assessments:** If you feel the school isn't capturing the full picture, request additional evaluations.
- **Include Relevant Context:** For example, if your child performs better in small groups than in a whole-class setting, that should be noted.

Your Play for This Chapter

Sit down with your child's Present Levels and ask yourself: Does this match the child I know? Is there anything missing? Are there areas where the language feels too vague or overly positive? If the answer to any of these questions is "yes," it's time to advocate for changes.

Remember, this section is your child's baseline. It's not just a snapshot; it's the foundation for their success. Don't let it be an afterthought.

With strong Present Levels, the rest of your child's IEP can stand strong.

CHAPTER 12

Transition Planning

Transition planning. Just reading those two words can make even the most seasoned parent of a child with an individualized education program (IEP) feel overwhelmed. It's no wonder because this is the part of the IEP process where we move beyond academics and into the uncharted territory of adulthood. Whether your children are aiming for college, a career, or greater independence in their daily life, transition planning is your opportunity to set the stage for their future success.

Unfortunately, the IEP transition plans I see on IEPs are some of the weakest parts of the IEP I read. If your child's transition plan feels more like a generic checkbox than a meaningful road map, you're not alone. Let's dig into what IDEA says about transition planning, what a great transition plan looks like, and how to avoid the common pitfalls that can derail this critical process.

What Does IDEA Say About Transition Planning?

The Individuals with Disabilities Education Act (IDEA) mandates that transition planning begins no later than the school year in which your child turns 16 years old. Some states wisely start earlier—at age 12 or 14—giving families more time to prepare for the significant shift that comes after high school. If your state doesn't start early, you can absolutely ask your IEP team to begin sooner. (Trust me, waiting until junior year is like trying to plan a wedding in a week. Don't do it!)

Transition planning isn't just about academics. It's about creating a comprehensive plan for life after high school, which IDEA refers to as "post-secondary goals." These goals must address three main areas:

- Education or Training (e.g., college, vocational school, or other post-secondary programs)
- Employment (e.g., part-time or full-time work, job training, internships)
- Independent Living (if appropriate for the students, including skills like managing money, navigating transportation, or living on their own)

IDEA emphasizes that these goals must be individualized, based on your child's strengths, preferences, and interests. Transition planning isn't about shoving your children into a pre-existing program: It's about building a road map that fits their unique abilities and dreams.

The Key Components of a Transition Plan

A strong transition plan has several essential elements. All states have their own standardized IEP template, and IEP writing software programs vary. What is on your child's IEP may not be in this exact order. Let's break them down.

Post-Secondary Goals

These are the long-term objectives for what your child wants to do after high school. They should be:

- **Measurable:** Instead of vague statements like "John will be successful," the goals should specify what success looks like. For example, "John will complete a two-year welding program at XYZ Community College" or "Maria will obtain part-time employment in a retail environment."
- **Based on Assessments:** Transition goals should be informed by age-appropriate transition assessments. These might include interest inventories, aptitude tests, or hands-on experiences like job shadowing.

Transition Services

This section outlines the supports, services, and activities your children will need to achieve their post-secondary goals. Examples include:

- Career counseling or job coaching
- Life skills training, such as cooking or managing finances
- Opportunities for internships, apprenticeships, or part-time jobs

These services should be specific and actionable—not vague promises like "explore career options."

Courses of Study

This is your children's academic road map. It should include the classes and programs they'll take in high school to prepare for their goals. For example:

- A student aiming for college might need advanced math and science classes.
- A student interested in auto mechanics might take vocational courses alongside core academics.

Annual Goals Related to Transition

Transition plans should include measurable annual goals. For example, if your children's post-secondary goal is to work in an office setting, their IEP might include a goal like, "By the end of the school year, Alex will demonstrate the ability to use spreadsheet software to complete assigned tasks with 90% accuracy."

Age of Majority

When your children reach the "age of majority" (usually 18), they gain the legal right to make decisions about their education. The IEP must address this milestone, including steps to prepare your child for self-advocacy or, if necessary, discussions about guardianship or supported decision-making.

Involvement of Outside Agencies

If your child will need support from outside organizations—like Vocational Rehabilitation, job training programs, or adult services—the IEP team should start coordinating with these agencies before graduation. This ensures a smoother transition and prevents gaps in services.

Start Early, Plan Thoroughly

While IDEA requires transition planning to begin by age 16, starting earlier can make a huge difference. By age 12 or 14, the IEP team can start exploring your children's interests and strengths, giving them time to develop the skills they'll need.

Early planning allows for:

- **Exposure to Different Careers:** Encourage your child to explore a variety of career paths through job shadowing, internships, or summer programs.
- **Skill Development:** Start working on independent living skills like budgeting, cooking, or using public transportation.
- **Course Alignment:** Ensure your children's high school courses align with their goals, whether that means taking advanced placement classes or enrolling in vocational training.

Common Pitfalls in Transition Planning

Despite its importance, transition planning is often one of the weakest sections of the IEP. Here's what to watch out for.

Generic Plans

Transition plans should be as unique as your child. If the plan feels like a copy-and-paste job, ask questions. For example, if your child dreams of working in the medical field but the plan says "explore career options," push for specifics like shadowing a nurse or visiting a hospital.

Ignoring Independent Living Skills

Schools often focus on academics or employment and overlook life skills. Even if your children plan to live at home, they'll still benefit from learning how to cook, clean, manage money, or schedule appointments.

Lack of Outside Agency Involvement

Schools commonly wait too long to involve outside agencies like Vocational Rehabilitation. If these agencies aren't looped in before graduation, your child could face gaps in support.

I cannot say this often enough or loudly enough: If you do not take ownership of your child's IEP transition plan, you will be offered the generic things the school offers everyone else. You are going to have to do the legwork on this, find programs, find ideas, and bring them to the table.

Advocates have a saying in this: "Food, filth and flowers." That tends to be the bulk of the transition programs our kids are offered. Either working in food service, cleaning and janitorial services, or fluff things like flower arranging.

I'm not knocking any of those career choices. But what if that is not what your child wants to do? You're going to have to network, search, ask and see what you can find. Otherwise, your child will be offered a spot in one of the food, filth, or flower programs. And if those programs can be matched up to your child's IEP goals, it will be very difficult to demonstrate that is not FAPE for your child.

How to Advocate for a Better Transition Plan

Here is how to advocate for a better transition plan:

1. Start with a Vision Statement

    Before diving into the IEP, work with your child to create a vision statement. This is a short description of what they want their life to look like after high school. For example:

    "By age 25, I want to work as a graphic designer, live in my own apartment, and take care of my dog."

2. Demand Specificity

   Every goal and service in the transition plan should be actionable and measurable. Instead of "learn job skills," push for something like "complete a six-week internship in the hospitality industry."

3. Get Creative

   If the school's programs don't align with your child's goals, think outside the box. Reach out to community organizations, local businesses, or even friends and family to create opportunities. Use what social capital you have, your network of friends and colleagues, to get something set up for your child.

4. Engage Outside Agencies Early

   Ask the IEP team to invite Vocational Rehabilitation or other agencies to meetings as early as possible. These organizations can provide valuable resources and support.

Transition planning is about more than just meeting IDEA's requirements. It's about empowering your child to step into adulthood with confidence and a clear sense of direction. While it's easy to feel overwhelmed, taking an active role in the process can make a huge difference.

Remember, this is your children's future we're planning. Let's make sure they're set up for success.

Your Play for This Chapter

1. Work with your child to create a vision statement. More information at **adayinourshoes .com/playbook**.

2. Review their current transition plan and identify gaps or vague language.

CHAPTER 13

IEP Goals and Objectives

Even though Present Levels is my favorite section of an individualized education program (IEP) and in my professional opinion, the most important section, it's IEP goals that usually get the most attention.

IEP goals are the road map for your children's progress, outlining what they should achieve within the year and the skills they'll work on. But let's be real; just slapping a few generic goals onto an IEP and calling it a day isn't enough. To truly serve their purpose, IEP goals need to be thoughtful, measurable, and uniquely tailored to your child's needs.

I often describe IEP goals as "part science, part art." The science lies in grounding the goals in data, evaluations, and the Present Levels of Performance (PLOP). The art? That's the finesse required to craft goals that are meaningful, relevant, and achievable.

In this chapter, we'll explore everything you need to know about IEP goals: what Individuals with Disabilities Education Act (IDEA) requires, who writes them, what makes a goal effective, and how to navigate disagreements. We'll break down good versus bad goals, introduce you to the SMART goals framework, and provide actionable steps to ensure your child's IEP sets them up for success.

The Legal Foundation: What IDEA Says About IEP Goals

The IDEA mandates that every IEP include measurable annual goals. These goals must address both:

1. **Academic Skills:** Areas like reading comprehension, math fluency, and writing proficiency
2. **Functional Skills:** Areas like social-emotional regulation, communication, self-advocacy, and daily living skills

The word *measurable* is key. A goal must be written in a way that allows both parents and educators to track progress. For example, a vague goal like "Sam will improve his reading" doesn't meet the standard. A measurable goal like "Sam will read a grade-level passage with 90% accuracy in four out of five trials" does.

Why Measurable Goals Matter

Measurable goals are important because they:

- Provide clear expectations for the team and your child.
- Allow for consistent progress monitoring.
- Enable accountability; if a goal isn't met, it's easier to identify gaps in support or services.

Who Writes IEP Goals?

In theory, IEP goals are written collaboratively by the IEP team. This includes:

- The special education teacher
- General education teachers
- Specialists like speech or occupational therapists
- Parents (that's you!)

In practice, many schools arrive at the IEP meeting with pre-written draft goals. While this can streamline the process, it's critical to remember that these are *drafts*. If a goal doesn't align with your child's needs, speak up.

If you feel confident, you can even bring your own draft goals to the meeting. This is perfectly acceptable and ensures that the discussion starts from a place that prioritizes your child's unique challenges.

Advocacy Tip: You can find an IEP goal bank with thousands of IEP goal ideas at **adayinourshoes.com/iep-goal-bank/** that you can browse anytime but certainly for ideas before an IEP meeting.

IEP Goals vs. Objectives

It's easy to confuse IEP goals with objectives (or benchmarks), so let's clarify:

- Goals are the big-picture targets. For example, "By June 2025, Alex will independently solve multi-step math word problems with 80% accuracy."
- Objectives are the smaller steps that lead to the goal. For example:
  - Solve single-step word problems with 90% accuracy.
  - Solve two-step problems with teacher support.
  - Independently solve three-step problems.

IDEA only requires objectives if your child is taking alternate assessments. However, objectives can be helpful for all students because they break goals into manageable steps. If you think objectives would benefit your child, don't hesitate to request them.

How Many Goals Should an IEP Include?

There's no one-size-fits-all answer to this question. The number of goals depends entirely on your child's needs.

Here are some guidelines:

- For children with multiple areas of need, there should be at least one goal for each area (e.g., academic, social-emotional, behavior, functional skills).
- Focus on quality over quantity. A handful of well-written, targeted goals is more effective than a laundry list of vague or unattainable goals.

If your team says, "We can only have X number of goals," ask them to show you where IDEA imposes that limit. IDEA does not require a specific number of IEP goals, nor does it prohibit the number of IEP goals. The IEP must be individualized, and that includes the number of goals.

SMART Goals: The Gold Standard

The SMART framework ensures that goals are:

- Specific: Clearly define what the goal is.
- Measurable: Include criteria for tracking progress.
- Achievable: Set realistic expectations based on your child's abilities.
- Relevant: Align with your child's unique needs.
- Time-bound: Specify a timeframe for achievement.

The following is an example of a bad goal:

"Ella will improve her writing skills."

- Why it's bad: It's vague and unmeasurable.

The following is an example of a SMART goal:

"By June 2025, Ella will independently write a five-sentence paragraph with proper punctuation in four out of five trials, as measured by teacher-made rubrics."

- Why it's good: It's specific, measurable, and tied to a clear timeline.

  Here is another example, this time of a reading goal:

- Bad: "Chris will get better at reading."
- Good: "By June 2025, Chris will read a grade-level passage at 100 words per minute with 95% accuracy in four out of five trials."

  Here is an example of a social skills goal:

- Bad: "Emma will be a good friend."
- Good: "By the end of the school year, Emma will initiate a peer interaction (e.g., asking to join a game) on three out of five opportunities as observed by the teacher."

Common IEP Goal Pitfalls

As you review your child's IEP, watch out for these red flags:

- **Vague Language:** Terms like "improve" or "increase" without specifics are problematic.
- **No Baseline Data:** Goals should stem from the PLOP. If there's no baseline, how can you measure progress?
- **Recycled Goals:** Goals shouldn't remain unchanged year after year. This could indicate a lack of progress or ineffective interventions.
- **Disappearing Goals:** Goals shouldn't vanish without explanation. Always ask why a goal has been removed.

FAQs About IEP Goals

- **What if the children not meet their IEP goals?** Not meeting IEP goals may be an indicator that a child is being denied FAPE. But this is one of those situations where a parent is really going to have to dig in and learn and try to target the issue. Remember, that not meeting a goal does not necessarily mean that the child did not make any progress at all. The goal may have been too aggressive to be accomplished in one year. It could mean that more or different supports are needed. More information is needed before a team can answer this question.
- **What's the point of an IEP if my child has the same goals every year?** This is a huge red flag that your **IEP is junk**. The whole point of having IEP goals specific to your child is to monitor progress. If you are seeing the same goals year after year, it's time to really engage in the process.

- **How many goals should there be on an IEP?** IDEA does not define this. Nor do any state regulations to my knowledge. IEPs are to be individualized so they will vary from child to child. There's a lot to consider: how many areas of need, how many hours in a day, the child's skill level, and so on. For some kids, you're just not going to be able to hit every need every day. As a parent, make sure you are participating in **the IEP process** so that your and your child's priorities are taken into account when deciding goals. And, know that at least per IDEA, there are no "have-tos" or "can'ts." I hear a lot of "We can't have more than six goals on an IEP." Their school district policy may state that or use it as a best practice, but again, IDEA makes no determination of how many goals there should be. Keep pushing if it's something you want.

- **My child's goals sometimes disappear from year to year. Is that normal?** Common? Yes. Normal, not really. Again, IEP goals are written so that parents and schools can measure progress. If a goal disappears, what does it mean? That the child has achieved it? Or did someone just make a clerical error? Is this not a priority anymore? It's okay to remove a goal from an IEP as long as the team is in agreement. A student's needs and priorities will change over time. But no, goals should not just disappear from an IEP at renewal time without explanation and agreement from the team.

- **Can parents submit IEP goal ideas?** Absolutely! Again, the IEP is meant to be a collaborative approach with your ideas and priorities in mind. Just remember that they are based on needs.

- **How do you know if a goal is measurable or appropriate?** Many IEP teams use the SMART IEP goal acronym. SMART stands for Specific, Measurable, Achievable, Relevant, and Time Bound.

- **What if there is a goal on the IEP that I don't want?** A parent's concerns and priorities should always be taken into consideration, but ultimately it is a team decision. If there is a goal on the IEP that is just not something you want your child to be working on, have the data ready to support your other priorities as well as some replacement goal ideas.

IEP goals are the cornerstone of your child's educational plan. When done well, they provide a clear path forward and hold the school accountable for your child's progress. When done poorly, they can leave your children spinning their wheels or worse, regressing.

Remember, IEPs are living documents. They're meant to grow and evolve as your child does. Don't settle for vague or inadequate goals. Advocate for goals that set your child up for success because they deserve nothing less.

Your Play for This Chapter

Take out your child's IEP and look at the goals. Are they measurable? Do they reflect progress? Use the accompanying worksheet to identify gaps and areas for improvement.

If you have a previous IEP, you should always compare IEPs year to year, especially the goals. After all, if there isn't improvement, why are we doing all of this?

CHAPTER 14

Special Education Services and Supplementary Aids

SDIs are the the "how" of your child's education plan. It's what your child "gets" as far as supports and services on their individualized education program (IEP). It's the section that parents want to advocate for the most often, or change the most often. Let me say this: Flipping straight to SDIs and advocating for change is getting ahead of yourself.

Why? Because Specially Designed Instructions (SDIs) are built on the foundation of evaluations, Present Levels, and goals. If those sections are flawed, the SDIs won't do what they're supposed to do. Or, the SDIs may not be right for your child if the earlier parts of the IEP are not correct. Here's an example: Let's say children have ADHD and struggle with reading. So, their IEP has accommodations for reading coming from an ADHD perspective. But what if the children were not evaluated for dyslexia and in fact is dyslexic? Then those ADHD accommodations will never help them become a better reader.

But SDIs are critically important. They represent the individualized support your child receives, which is the heart of special education. Without solid SDIs, the rest of the IEP is just a pile of paper.

What Is Specially Designed Instruction?

Let's start with the basics: SDIs are *the* defining feature of special education under the Individuals with Disabilities Education Act (IDEA). If your children have an IEP, they are receiving special education, and that means they are entitled to SDIs.

Here's how SDIs differ from other supports in the IEP:

- **Special Education Services:** These are the programs or therapies your child receives, like speech therapy, occupational therapy, or one-on-one reading instruction.

- **Specially Designed Instruction (SDI):** This is the *how*. It's the method or adaptation of teaching to meet your child's specific needs.

Think of SDI as the custom-tailored approach to delivering instruction. For example:

- **Adapting the *content*:** Simplifying complex material for better comprehension
- **Adjusting the *methodology*:** Using hands-on activities or visual aids for a child who struggles with verbal instructions
- **Modifying the *delivery*:** Teaching in a small group or one-on-one setting instead of the general classroom

What About Supplementary Aids and Services?

Closely related to SDIs are supplementary aids and services. These are the tools and supports that help your child access the curriculum and participate in the school environment.

Examples include:

- **Assistive Technology:** Devices like text-to-speech software, communication boards, or adaptive keyboards
- **Behavioral Supports:** Positive behavior plans, sensory breaks, or social stories
- **Environmental Modifications:** Preferential seating, quiet spaces, or noise-canceling headphones
- **Collaborative Supports:** Scheduled time for teachers and specialists to meet and coordinate

If SDIs are the "how," supplementary aids are the "what" that make the "how" possible.

Examples of Strong SDIs and Supplementary Aids

To paint a clearer picture, here are some examples of effective SDIs and supplementary aids:

- **Instructional SDI:** "The student will receive explicit, step-by-step instruction with visual aids for multi-step math problems."
- **Behavioral SDI:** "The student will use a break card system to request sensory breaks when overwhelmed."
- **Assistive Technology:** "The student will use a speech-to-text app to complete written assignments longer than five sentences."

- **Environmental Support:** "Noise-canceling headphones will be available during tests and independent work."

Each of these examples is specific, measurable, and directly tied to a child's needs.

What Should Be in the SDI Section of an IEP?

The SDI section should answer the following questions clearly and specifically:

1. What are the services?

    For example: "The student will receive 30 minutes of Orton-Gillingham (OG) reading intervention, four times per week."
2. Who provides them?

    Is it a special education teacher, a speech therapist, or a paraprofessional?
3. Where will they be delivered?

    In the general education classroom, a resource room, or a therapy setting?
4. How often and for how long?

    The frequency and duration should be explicitly stated, like "30 minutes daily for the entire school year."
5. What is the purpose?

    Each SDI should tie directly to one of your child's IEP goals.

Common Issues with SDIs

As much as I wish all SDI sections are flawless, they rarely are. Here are the most common issues I encounter:

1. Vague Descriptions

    If an SDI says, "The student will receive math support as needed," that's a problem. What does "as needed" mean? Who decides when it's needed? Always push for clarity and specificity.
2. Missing Services

    Shockingly, I often see IEPs where critical services are completely left out. For example, a child with dyslexia might have goals for reading but no evidence-based reading program listed in their SDIs.
3. Failure to Name Programs

    Schools sometimes avoid naming specific programs in the IEP. But there's no law against naming them. In fact, listing the program, like Wilson Reading or Orton-Gillingham (OG), holds the school accountable for using an evidence-based intervention delivered with fidelity.

4. Onus on the Student

Some IEPs use phrasing like, "The student will have access to a quiet space for breaks." That sounds nice, but if the child has to self-advocate for the break, it may not happen. Does your child have the skills to ask for what they need?

Tips for Parents

Reading the SDI section of an IEP can be daunting, but it's critical to do so carefully. Here's how to approach it:

1. Match SDIs to Goals

Every goal in the IEP should have a corresponding SDI or service. If a goal says, "The student will improve reading fluency," there should be a specific intervention listed, like "30 minutes of Orton-Gillingham (OG) instruction, three times per week."

2. Push for Evidence-Based Practices

Don't settle for vague promises of "support." Ask for interventions that are research-based and proven to work for your child's needs.

3. Avoid Overloading

More is not always better. The goal is to provide the *right* amount of the *right* supports and not to pile on services that aren't needed or effective.

4. Be Specific About Delivery

Who is responsible for implementing each SDI? If it's a paraprofessional, does that person have the training to deliver the intervention effectively?

5. Focus on Independence

Good SDIs should help your child become more independent over time. For example, instead of always relying on an aide, your child might learn to use a planner to stay organized.

Accommodations vs. Modifications vs. SDI

The world of special education is full of terms that seem interchangeable at first glance, but they carry distinct meanings and serve different purposes. Among the most commonly confused are accommodations, modifications, and SDI. Understanding the nuances among these three elements is crucial for ensuring that your child receives the support they need to succeed in school.

Accommodations: Altering the "How" of Learning

Accommodations are adjustments to the environment, materials, or instructional methods that allow a student to access the general education curriculum without changing the curriculum's content or expectations. The purpose of accommodations is to provide a level playing field. They are not intended to give an advantage or lower academic standards, but rather to help the student demonstrate what they know and can do.

For example, children with dyslexia might be given access to audiobooks. The content of the book remains unchanged, but the way they consume the material is adapted to their needs. Similarly, a student with ADHD might receive extended time on tests to account for challenges with focus and processing speed.

Accommodations address barriers to access rather than altering the actual curriculum. Students are expected to meet the same grade-level standards as their peers but with additional tools or strategies in place to help them succeed.

Modifications: Adjusting the "What" of Learning

Modifications, unlike accommodations, do change the expectations or content. They involve adjusting the curriculum to better fit the individual needs of the student. Modifications are typically used when students cannot meet the same grade-level standards as their peers, even with accommodations in place.

For instance, students might be given a simplified reading assignment with fewer pages or vocabulary words than the rest of the class. In math, they might work on basic arithmetic while their classmates tackle algebra. Modifications ensure students are still learning and progressing, but the goals are tailored to their current abilities.

The key distinction here is that modifications alter the educational expectations. The student is no longer working toward the same standards as their peers. While this can be beneficial for students with significant disabilities, it may also impact their ability to receive a standard high school diploma or move easily between educational tracks.

SDI: Individualized Teaching

SDI refers to teaching methods and strategies that are customized to meet the unique needs of a student with a disability. Unlike accommodations or modifications, SDI is a direct service provided by a special education teacher or specialist. It focuses on how the content is taught rather than what is taught or how it is accessed.

For example, a student with a learning disability in reading might receive one-on-one instruction in decoding and fluency using evidence-based strategies. A child with autism may work with a specialist to develop social skills through role-playing and direct instruction.

SDI is a cornerstone of special education and is required under the Individuals with Disabilities Education Act (IDEA). It is inherently flexible and tailored, designed to address the specific challenges and strengths of each individual student.

Comparing Accommodations, Modifications, and SDI

While accommodations, modifications, and SDI serve different purposes, they share the common goal of supporting students with disabilities to succeed in their educational journey. Table 14.1 shows a quick comparison.

TABLE 14.1   **Accommodations, Modifications, and SDI**

Feature	Accommodations	Modifications	Specially Designed Instruction (SDI)
Purpose	Provide equal access	Alter expectations	Individualized teaching strategies
Changes to Content?	No	Yes	No
Goal	Access grade-level standards	Meet individualized goals	Address specific educational needs
Delivery	General education setting	General education setting	Often in a special education setting
Examples	Extra time, audiobooks	Simplified assignments	Direct instruction in specific skills

Despite their differences, accommodations, modifications, and SDI often work together to support a student's learning. A student may receive accommodations and SDI simultaneously, such as using audiobooks (accommodation) while working one-on-one with a reading specialist (SDI). Similarly, a student with modifications in place might also benefit from SDI to address specific skill deficits.

For instance, children with significant learning disabilities might have their math assignments modified to focus on basic arithmetic (modification), receive visual aids to support understanding (accommodation), and work with a special education teacher on foundational math concepts (SDI).

The overlap among these supports highlights the flexibility of proper special education planning. Each element is chosen based on the individual needs of students, ensuring they have the opportunity to make progress and achieve their potential.

SDI and supplementary aids are what move your child forward. They're what turn goals into action. Without clear, well-crafted SDIs, your child's IEP is just a document. But with the right supports, your child can thrive.

Take the time to read the SDI section carefully. Ask questions. Push for specifics. And never stop advocating for what your child needs to succeed.

Your Play for This Chapter

- Read the SDI section of your child's IEP carefully.
- Look for vague language or missing details.
- Research evidence-based practices for your child's specific needs.

CHAPTER 15

IEP-Related Services

This chapter covers IEP-related services. These services are more than just add-ons; they're often the game-changer that bridges the gap between children's challenges and their ability to succeed in school.

When it comes to individualized education programs (IEPs), related services are the unsung heroes. They're often tucked away in the middle of the document, overshadowed by goals and Specially Designed Instruction (SDIs). Yet, these services can be the difference between your child merely getting by and truly thriving.

Many parents flip straight to this section, eager to see how much support their child will receive. While it's natural to focus on quantity, the quality and specificity of related services are what really matter.

What Are IEP-Related Services?

Under the Individuals with Disabilities Education Act (IDEA), related services are defined as supportive services necessary for children with disabilities to benefit from their special education program. They aren't optional or "nice-to-haves." If your children require them to access their education, they are an essential part of their right to a Free Appropriate Public Education (FAPE).

Here's how IDEA describes related services:

"Transportation and such developmental, corrective, and other supportive services as are required to assist a child with a disability to benefit from special education."

This definition is intentionally broad, covering a wide range of supports. Related services include (but are not limited to):

- Speech-language pathology
- Audiology services

- Occupational Therapy (OT)
- Physical Therapy (PT)
- Counseling and psychological services
- Parent counseling and training
- Transportation
- Orientation and mobility services
- Assistive technology
- Medical services for diagnostic or evaluation purposes

In simpler terms, related services help remove the barriers that prevent your children from participating in and benefiting from their education.

Common Types of Related Services

1. **Speech and Language Therapy**
   This service addresses communication challenges, such as articulation, language comprehension, and expressive language.

   Example: A speech therapist works with a child on forming complete sentences, using picture cards or a communication device.

2. **Occupational Therapy (OT)**
   OT focuses on fine motor skills, sensory regulation, and daily living tasks.

   Example: A child practices tying their shoes or using a pencil grip to improve handwriting.

3. **Physical Therapy (PT)**
   PT targets gross motor skills, mobility, and physical independence.

   Example: A student learns exercises to improve balance and coordination, enabling them to navigate stairs independently.

4. **Counseling Services**
   These services support emotional regulation, coping strategies, and social skills.

   Example: A weekly small-group session helps students practice conflict resolution skills in real-world scenario.

5. **Behavioral Support**
   Behavioral services address challenges that disrupt learning, often through Functional Behavior Assessments (FBA) and Behavior Intervention Plans (BIPs).

   Example: A behavior specialist teaches a student how to use a break card to self-regulate when overwhelmed.

6. Transportation

   For students with mobility challenges or safety concerns, transportation services ensure they can get to and from school.

   Example: A wheelchair-accessible bus picks up students at their door.

7. Parent Counseling and Training

   This service helps parents understand their child's needs and how to support them at home.

   Example: A training session shows parents how to use a child's speech-generating device during family meals.

How Are Related Services Determined?

The IEP team decides which related services your child needs based on evaluations, assessments, and observations. Here's the four-step process:

Step 1: Evaluation and Assessment

   A thorough evaluation identifies your child's specific challenges and needs.

   Example: A speech-language evaluation uncovers difficulty with expressive language and auditory processing.

Step 2: Identifying Barriers

   The team determines how these challenges impact your child's ability to learn or access the curriculum.

   Example: Does poor motor coordination make it difficult for your child to complete written assignments?

Step 3: Developing Goals

   Related services should tie directly to your child's IEP goals.

   Example: If a child has a goal to write a legible paragraph, occupational therapy might focus on improving grip strength and pencil control.

Step 4: Writing Services Into the IEP

   Every related service should include:

- Frequency: How often the service will be provided
- Duration: How long each session will last
- Location: Where the service will take place (e.g., classroom therapy room)
- Delivery Method: Whether it's individual or group-based.

   Example: "Occupational therapy, 30 minutes, twice a week, in a one-on-one setting."

Common Issues in Related Services

The following are five common issues that arise when documenting related services:

1. Vague Language

   Watch out for phrases like "as needed" or "when appropriate." These leave too much room for interpretation. Push for specificity.

   Example: Replace "speech therapy as needed" with "speech therapy, 30 minutes, twice a week, in a group of no more than four students."

2. Consultative Services

   Some services are marked as "consultative," meaning the specialist advises the teacher rather than working directly with your child. While consultative services can be appropriate in certain situations, they're not a substitute for direct intervention.

3. Insufficient Services

   Schools may offer the bare minimum to save resources. If you believe your child needs more, gather evidence to support your request (e.g., private evaluations, work samples).

4. Overlooked Needs

   Related services commonly exclude critical supports like mental health counseling or sensory integration. If your child has unmet needs, bring them up during the IEP meeting.

5. Failure to Deliver Services
   Even if services are written into the IEP, they might not always be implemented. Stay vigilant by tracking your child's schedule and progress reports.

Tricky Math and IEP Related Services

"Tricky math" is a trend I'm seeing in recent years that is an issue with related services. I felt it warranted more explanation than a bullet point.

Here's what I mean by tricky math. Most parents understand the statement, "Student will receive 30 minutes a week of small group OT services for sensory and fine motor skills." However, in recent years, I have seen more statements like, "Student will receive 600 minutes of small group OT services this school year."

With all the information and stress during an IEP meeting, the concept of 600 minutes is not dissected or examined enough. A school year is typically 40 weeks. So, 600 minutes is only 15 minutes a week, even fewer if your school uses a six-day cycle system instead of calendar days.

If your last IEP said 30 minutes a week, and this one says 600 minutes a year, your child' OT time was just cut in half! If your school team uses this to calculate related service minutes, don't be afraid to pause the meeting while you do the math.

Private vs. School-Based Services

While schools are required to provide related services, they may not always meet the full scope of your child's needs. This is where private services can fill the gap. Many parents supplement their child's IEP with private services, paid for with insurance or out of pocket. These are why you may need to turn to private services:

- **Caseloads:** School therapists often juggle large caseloads, limiting the time they can dedicate to each student.
- **Expertise:** Private therapists may have specialized training in specific techniques or conditions.
- **Flexibility:** Private services often allow for more individualized attention and longer sessions.

These are the financial considerations:

- **Insurance Coverage:** Check if your health plan covers therapies like OT or counseling.
- **Nonprofit Resources:** Some organizations offer sliding-scale fees or free services for families in need.

Even temporary private services can provide a "boost," helping your child make faster progress.

Examples of Strong IEP Language for Related Services

The following are examples of using strong IEP language for related services:

1. Speech Therapy:

    "Speech-language therapy, 30 minutes, twice a week, in a group of no more than three students, focusing on articulation and expressive language."
2. Occupational Therapy:

    "OT sessions, 20 minutes, three times per week, to improve fine motor skills and handwriting legibility."
3. Behavioral Support:

    "A behavior specialist will provide weekly one-to-one sessions to implement self-regulation strategies as part of the student's BIP."
4. Parent Training:

    "Monthly parent counseling sessions to teach strategies for managing sensory challenges at home."

Taking Action

As a parent, you have the right—and the responsibility—to ensure your child's related services are appropriate and effective.

Related services are more than just a section in the IEP; they're the tools that empower your child to succeed. With the right supports in place, your child can overcome barriers and achieve meaningful progress.

Let's make sure that happens.

Your Play for This Chapter

1. Review the IEP: Look for vague language, missing services, or insufficient frequency.
2. Gather Data: Use evaluations, work samples, and observations to back up your requests.
3. Explore Private Options: If school-based services fall short, consider supplementing with private therapy if that is an option for you.
4. Ask Questions: Don't hesitate to ask for clarification or push for changes during the IEP meeting.

CHAPTER 16

Supports
for School Personnel

W hen flipping through the pages of your child's individualized education program
(IEP), it's easy to zero in on the goals, Specially Designed Instructions (SDIs), and
related services. But there's one section that often gets overlooked: Supports for
School Personnel. Let me tell you, this section is crucial, and it's often the missing link in
ensuring your child's IEP is successfully implemented. If the teachers, aides, and other staff
working with your child don't have the proper training and resources, how can we expect
them to implement the IEP with fidelity? The short answer: we can't.

Let's dig into what this section is, why it's important, and how to make sure it works for
your child. Spoiler: it's more than just promising that someone will "get training."

What Is the "Supports for School Personnel" Section?

The Supports for School Personnel section of the IEP is where the team outlines the
training, resources, and tools school staff need to effectively implement the IEP. This
includes everyone who interacts with your child: general education teachers, special education teachers, paraprofessionals (aides), therapists, bus drivers, cafeteria staff, and even
recess monitors.

In short, this section is about ensuring the adults responsible for your child's education are equipped to meet their needs. And let's be honest: Most teachers and aides don't
have specific training in every disability, behavior plan, or assistive technology. Without
this section, they're left to figure it out on their own, which isn't fair to them or your child.

Why Is This Section Important?

Imagine your child has a Behavior Intervention Plan (BIP) that requires specific de-escalation
strategies when they become anxious. Now picture the classroom teacher, aide, or bus

driver trying to manage a meltdown without any training on those techniques. What happens? The plan isn't implemented correctly—or at all—and your child's behavior escalates. It's a lose-lose situation for everyone involved.

The Supports for School Personnel section is the safety net. It ensures that everyone working with your child has the knowledge, tools, and confidence to carry out the IEP effectively. It's also a way to create consistency throughout your child's day. Whether your child is in the classroom, cafeteria, or playground, the adults around them should know how to meet their needs.

What Should Be Included?

Let's get specific about what should go into this section. Vague promises like "Staff will receive training" don't cut it. Here's what a strong Supports for School Personnel section should include:

1. Training on Specific Disabilities

    If your child has autism, ADHD, sensory needs, or another disability, staff may need training tailored to those challenges. For example:
    • Creating a sensory-friendly classroom for a child with sensory processing issues

    • Understanding executive functioning deficits for a child with ADHD

    • Learning how to use visual schedules or social stories for a child on the autism spectrum

2. Training on Behavior Plans

    Behavior plans are only as good as the people implementing them. Staff need to understand the specific strategies in your child's BIP, such as:
    • De-escalation techniques

    • Positive reinforcement strategies

    • How to handle meltdowns or aggressive behaviors without escalating the situation

3. Training on Assistive Technology (AT)

    If your child uses AT—such as a communication device or text-to-speech software—staff need hands-on training. The device won't help if it's gathering dust on a shelf because no one knows how to use it.

4. Collaboration Time for Staff

    If your children have multiple specialists, they need time to collaborate. For instance:
    • A speech therapist and occupational therapist working together on sensory strategies to improve classroom participation.

    • Regular team meetings to discuss progress and adjust strategies as needed.

5. Access to Specialists

   Sometimes, staff need guidance from outside experts. For example:
   - A behavior specialist consulting on a complex BIP
   - An audiologist training staff on how to use FM systems for a child with hearing impairments

6. Paraprofessional Support and Training

   If your child has a one-to-one aide, that person needs specific training. This might include:
   - Academic support strategies
   - Behavior management techniques
   - Communication methods for non-verbal students

7. Environmental Modifications

   Staff may need support to create a classroom environment that works for your child. This could include:
   - Setting up a quiet corner for sensory breaks
   - Using alternative seating like wobble stools or therapy balls

8. Ongoing Support

   One-time training isn't enough. The IEP should include opportunities for staff to receive ongoing training and refreshers throughout the year.

Common Mistakes to Watch For

More often than not, the IEPs that I see are incomplete or weak. This is where you can show your support for not just your child, but help teachers get the support they need to implement IEPs.

1. Vague Language

   If the IEP says, "Staff will receive training," but doesn't specify what kind, who will provide it, or when it will happen, that's a problem. The IEP needs to be specific.

2. Forgetting Key Staff

   Your child interacts with more than just the classroom teacher. Don't forget about aides, bus drivers, lunch staff, and recess monitors. They need training, too.

3. Assuming Staff Already Know What to Do

   Just because someone works in education doesn't mean they've been trained on your child's specific needs. If your child's needs are unique, staff will likely need additional training.

4. Lack of Follow-Through

   Even the best-written supports are useless if they're not implemented. Follow up to ensure the training and supports are actually happening.

How to Advocate for Stronger Supports

If you feel the supports in the IEP are too vague—or missing entirely—here's what you can do:

1. Request Documentation

   Ask the school to document when and how staff received training. This holds the school accountable and ensures follow-through.

2. Propose Specific Supports

   Come to the table with ideas. For example:
   - "I found a webinar on sensory processing that might help the team."
   - "The local autism center offers free training sessions for schools. Can I reach out to them?"

3. Follow Up

   Check in regularly to ensure the supports are in place. Don't be afraid to ask for updates or additional training if needed.

4. Use Data

   If you notice gaps in implementation, document them. For example:
   - "I noticed that the behavior strategies weren't used during the incident on Tuesday. Can we revisit this with the team?"

Advocacy Tips

Here are some ideas that usually work to get this section of your IEP changed or built up.

Do the Legwork for Them

Schools are overwhelmed, and sometimes they say no to requests because they don't know where to start. Help them out by doing some of the legwork. For example:

- "I've contacted the local Epilepsy Foundation, and they're willing to provide training. Can I set this up for you?"

Be Collaborative

Approach the conversation with a collaborative tone. Instead of demanding training, frame it as a way to help everyone succeed.

The Supports for School Personnel section isn't just about helping teachers and staff: It's about helping your child. When school personnel are well-trained and supported, they can implement the IEP more effectively. This leads to better outcomes for your child and less stress for everyone involved.

With strong Supports for School Personnel in place, you're not just helping the adults in the room; instead, you're setting your child up for success.

Your Play for This Chapter

Take a close look at this section of your child's IEP. Ask yourself:

- Are the supports specific and detailed?
- Do they address all the staff who interact with your child?
- Are they realistic and actionable?

If the answer to any of these questions is no, it's time to advocate for stronger supports.

CHAPTER 17

Extended School Year (ESY)

Extended School Year (ESY) is one of those terms that gets thrown around in individualized education program (IEP) meetings, and many parents don't fully understand what it means or if their child qualifies for it. Sometimes, schools are vague about who qualifies and what services are available, which leaves parents confused and frustrated. While not every IEP student qualifies for ESY, it's important for parents to know what it is, how your child can qualify, and what to do if you disagree with the school about eligibility or programming.

First, ESY is not just "summer school." It's a specific set of services designed to prevent your children from losing the skills they've worked so hard to gain. So, if you've ever walked out of an IEP meeting wondering why ESY wasn't even discussed—or worse, why your child was denied—this chapter is for you.

What Is ESY?

ESY services are special education services provided *beyond the regular school year*. Yes, in most cases that means summer programs. Unlike summer school, which is usually about catching kids up or helping them pass a class, ESY is designed to help students maintain their skills. It's about preventing what's called *regression*, which is when children lose the skills they've gained during the school year because of an extended break, like summer vacation. I have had clients who have ESY services after school and weekends, because the traditional school calendar and hours were not enough to provide them what they need.

ESY services can take place during summer, but they can also be offered during other breaks in the school year, like winter break or spring break. The key here is that ESY is all about maintaining progress and not making new gains. So, if your children are at risk of losing ground without extra support during school breaks, they might qualify for ESY.

How Does a Child Qualify for ESY?

Qualifying for ESY isn't as simple as asking for it or checking off a box. The Individuals with Disabilities Education Act (IDEA) doesn't spell out specific eligibility criteria for ESY, which means that states and school districts have a lot of flexibility. That also means the decision can sometimes feel subjective, which can be frustrating for parents.

Here's what you need to know: ESY is based on your child's individual needs. The IEP team (that includes you!) decides if your child qualifies based on several factors. *You should familiarize yourself with your state's specific special education regulations because some state regulations state that ESY is only for regression.*

Some key things they'll consider are:

- **Regression and Recoupment:** This is the most common reason for ESY. The school will look at whether your child has a history of significant regression—meaning they lose skills during school breaks—and how long it takes them to recoup or regain those skills once school starts again. If it takes your children an unusually long time to get back to where they were, they might qualify for ESY.

- **Severity of the Disability:** Children with more severe disabilities or complex needs may be more likely to qualify for ESY because the risk of regression is higher.

- **Emerging Skills:** If your children are on the verge of mastering a critical skill (like learning to read, walk, or communicate more effectively), the IEP team may decide that they need ESY to keep that momentum going. Losing ground on an emerging skill can be particularly damaging.

- **Self-Sufficiency:** ESY can also be offered if losing skills could impact your child's ability to maintain independence. For example, if your children are working on self-care skills like toileting or dressing, losing progress could make them more dependent on others.

- **Behavioral Concerns:** If your child struggles with behavior or emotional regulation, and breaks from school make these behaviors worse, ESY might be needed to help maintain progress in managing these challenges.

- **Other Factors:** Some schools consider other things like the availability of home support, how much progress your child made during the school year, and whether they use assistive technology that requires ongoing instruction.

It's important to note that ESY is not about making progress; it's about maintaining the skills your child already has. If the school tells you that your children don't need ESY because they won't be learning anything new during the summer, that's a misunderstanding of how ESY works. The goal is to avoid backsliding.

Some states focus heavily on regression and recoupment as the primary criteria for determining eligibility for ESY services. These states tend to emphasize whether students are likely to lose skills over school breaks and how long it takes them to recover those skills (recoupment) once school resumes.

Here are some examples of states that focus predominantly on regression and recoupment for ESY eligibility:

- **Pennsylvania:** The Pennsylvania Department of Education focuses on a student's risk of regression and the time it takes to recoup lost skills as the primary criterion for ESY. Other factors may be considered, but regression is the key factor.
- **New York:** In New York, ESY eligibility is typically based on regression and recoupment, especially for students with more severe disabilities who are more likely to experience a loss of skills during breaks.
- **Texas:** Texas also focuses on regression and recoupment as its main criteria for ESY services, stating that ESY is primarily for students who risk significant skill loss during extended breaks.
- **Georgia:** Georgia's Department of Education guidelines emphasize the risk of regression and the time needed for recoupment when determining ESY eligibility. Regression/recoupment is a major consideration though the state does allow for other factors.

While many states have regression and recoupment as primary factors, some states, like California and New Jersey, also consider additional factors beyond just regression, such as the severity of the disability, the importance of skill maintenance, and emerging skills.

Advocacy Tip: Even if your state places a heavy emphasis on regression, IDEA does not restrict ESY to just regression and recoupment criteria. You can advocate for your child by emphasizing other factors allowed under federal law, such as emerging skills, behavioral issues, or the need for self-sufficiency.

What Programs Are Available for ESY?

The exact type of ESY services your child receives can vary widely depending on your child's needs and your school district's resources. ESY doesn't always look like traditional classroom instruction. Here are some of the types of programs you might see offered:

- **Direct Instruction:** This is probably the most familiar type of ESY, where your child goes to school for part of the summer (or another break) to receive instruction. It's usually a shorter day and fewer weeks than the regular school year, but it's still structured teaching. I call this the school's "canned program."
- **Related Services:** Some students might not need academic instruction but might qualify for services like speech therapy, OT, or PT to maintain their progress. These can be provided at school or sometimes even at home or in the community.
- **Home-Based Services:** For students who can't attend school for ESY, the district might offer services at home. This could be anything from tutoring to therapy sessions, depending on your child's needs.

- **Community-Based Services:** Some districts offer community-based learning experiences, especially for older students working on independent living or vocational skills. For example, your children might go to a job training site or practice life skills in a community setting as part of their ESY services.
- **Hybrid Models:** In some cases, ESY might involve a combination of different services. Your child might get direct instruction in some areas (like reading) and home-based support in others (like behavior or life skills).

Here's the key: The program should be tailored to your child's specific needs. If your children qualify for ESY, the IEP team must decide what services and supports are necessary to help them maintain their skills during the break. And it's not a one-size-fits-all situation. ESY could be a few weeks of instruction, a few hours of therapy, or a mix of both; it depends on what's needed to prevent regression.

You are not required to attend the school's canned program. However, that doesn't mean that they hand out all these free passes to therapeutic day camps either. If you find an ESY program for your child, ask yourself this:

- Why is this program appropriate for my children and their educational needs?
- Why is the school's canned program not appropriate for my child and their educational needs?

What If You Disagree About ESY?

It wouldn't be an IEP meeting without at least the possibility of disagreement, right? If you think your children need ESY and the IEP team doesn't agree, or if they qualify but you're not happy with the program offered, you have the following options:

- **Ask for Data:** Decisions about ESY should be based on data, that is things like past performance, progress reports, and assessments of your child's skills before and after breaks. If the team says your child doesn't need ESY, ask for the data that support that decision. Was there a formal regression/recoupment analysis done? Did the team monitor your child's skills after winter or spring break?
- **Provide Your Own Data:** You can also provide data from outside sources. If your child receives therapy or tutoring outside of school, and that professional has seen a pattern of regression during breaks, bring those data to the table. You can also share observations from home. If your child struggles more after school breaks, document that and share it with the team.
- **Document Disagreements in Writing:** If you disagree with the team members' decision about ESY, ask for a Prior Written Notice (PWN) that explains why they are refusing to provide services or why they've proposed a particular program. This is your official record, and it's important to have a paper trail.

- **Consider Mediation or Due Process:** If you've tried everything and still can't get the team to agree on ESY, you can file for mediation or due process. This is a more formal process, but sometimes it's necessary if the school isn't following the law or considering your child's needs appropriately.

ESY services are helpful for some students, especially if your child struggles with regression during school breaks. But qualifying for ESY isn't always easy, and it often feels like a battle to get the school to agree. Knowing what the law says, what data to look for, and how to advocate for your child is key to making sure they get the support they need.

Bonus Advocacy Tip: One tip I always tell parents: Keep data over the holidays. I know, I know. It's Thanksgiving, it's Christmas, who wants to keep IEP data now? But make a note of where your children are as far as progress and whatever skill you're concerned about. Then check in again in the beginning of January. Where are they? Did they regress? Check in again after MLK weekend. Where are they now? How long did recoupment take? These few pieces of data might just be the push that you need to get an ESY program for your child.

Whether it's keeping up with academics, maintaining behavioral progress, or holding on to those hard-earned functional skills, ESY is all about giving your child the best chance to succeed when the regular school year resumes. So, don't be afraid to ask for it, push for data, and keep advocating if you believe your child would benefit from ESY.

Your Play for This Chapter

Think about your child's ESY program. Let's be honest: ESY programs disrupt summer fun. It often changes a family's vacation schedule. So if you're going to disrupt your entire household's summer, your ESY program should be meaningful. Is it? And if it's not, what are you going to do about it?

CHAPTER 18

Placement and Least Restrictive Environment

U sually near the end of your individualized education program (IEP), there are two sections, often together—Placement and Progress Monitoring.

Just because they are near the end of the IEP doesn't make them any less important.

Placement is our child's day. It's where they are, and who they're with. Placement is the picture we get in our heads when we think about our kids at school.

Remember—IEPs have a defined process. Some places call it four or five steps, others seven. I'm in the camp who says five steps. Placement and progress monitoring are both, by Individuals with Disabilities Education Act (IDEA) definition at the end of the IEP process.

Let's review.

1. Evaluations and Eligibility
2. Goals.
3. Support and Services, Interventions, and Specially Designed Instructions (SDIs)
4. Placement: Placement is AFTER goals and supports. Per Individuals with Disabilities Education Act (IDEA), the team is to look at the IEP as it is written and ask, "What placement is best suited to implement this IEP?"
5. Progress Monitoring: That's covered in Chapter 26.

Think of it this way: Supports and services drive placement, not the other way around. I once had a client who was unhappy with her child's placement for a lot of reasons, mostly related to the related services her child was receiving. I kept trying to instill in her that the placement facility's responsibility is to implement the IEP as written, but she wasn't grasping it.

At one point, she said to me, "The whole reason I wanted him in this placement is because they give OT three times a week."

I said to her, "If he needs OT three times a week, we work on getting that in his IEP and then the placement has to provide it."

Placement is where your child's IEP will be implemented.

Where will your child spend their day? Will they be in a general education classroom, a special education setting, or something in between? And, once they're placed, how will you know if they're actually making progress?

Placement decisions go hand-in-hand with progress monitoring. You need to know not just where your children are learning, but whether they're learning effectively. The data should tell you that. But what does data reporting actually look like, and how can you use it to make sure your child's placement is working for them?

Let's unpack this, starting with placement decisions and how they are made, and then we'll dive into how progress monitoring should be done to keep you informed and your child on track.

What Is Placement in the IEP?

In special education, placement refers to the educational setting in which your children will receive their instruction and services. Placement goes hand in hand with Least Restrictive Environment (LRE), which is just fancy talk for making sure your children are educated alongside their non-disabled peers as much as possible while still meeting their needs. IDEA is clear that kids with disabilities should only be removed from general education settings if their needs can't be met there even with supplementary aids and services.

So, where might your child be placed? Here are some common options:

- **General Education Classroom (Full Inclusion):** Your children are in a regular classroom with their non-disabled peers for most or all of the day. They may receive special education services and accommodations while in this setting.

- **Resource Room (Partial Inclusion):** Your children spend part of the day in the general education classroom and part of the day in a special education setting (the resource room) for targeted instruction in areas where they need extra help, like reading or math.

- **Self-Contained Classroom:** This is a classroom where all students have IEPs and receive specialized instruction. Your children might spend the entire day or just part of the day here, depending on their needs.

- **Out-of-District Placement:** Sometimes, a child's needs are so unique that the public school district cannot meet them. In this case, the school may place your child in a specialized private school or another educational program.

- **Homebound Instruction:** In rare cases, children may receive their education at home, usually due to medical needs.

Remember, placement is not set in stone. It should evolve based on your child's progress, needs, and what the data tell you.

How Are IEP Placement Decisions Made?

Placement decisions are made by the IEP team, which includes you, the parent. Legally, placement decisions should come after your child's IEP goals and services are written. In other words, the team first identifies what supports and services your child needs to make progress and then decides where those services can be delivered most effectively.

Remember, supports, services, and interventions drive placement, not the other way around.

Here's a simple breakdown of how placement decisions should happen:

1. **Write the IEP Goals:** What are the specific, measurable goals your child will work on over the course of the year?
2. **Identify the Services:** What services will your child need to meet those goals (e.g., speech therapy, occupational therapy, behavioral support)?
3. **Choose the Placement:** Now that the goals and services are clear, the team decides where your child's needs can be met. The LRE is the goal, but the team should consider where your children will thrive, not just where they'll fit.

A common mistake is that schools sometimes reverse this process by suggesting a placement before writing the IEP. If the school members starts with "We think your child needs to be in the self-contained classroom" before they even look at the goals, stop them. That's not how it works. You write the goals first and then decide the placement that will best support achieving those goals.

Parents also make this mistake. They seek a specific placement because of what interventions are provided there. You add the interventions to the IEP first!

Another common mistake is that some parents and schools mistakenly think that children has to try every setting in the LRE continuum. They do not. The team should consider the continuum, but you are not required to try each stop along the way. In my experience, schools do not hand parents a list of placement options to choose from. Remember what I said earlier about that violating the "Individualized" tenet of IEPs? If a parent thinks their child will need an out-of-district placement, the onus is on them to do the research. Ask the school and it may give you some placements to look at. They also will then know that you are pursuing an out-of-district placement (read: expensive) for your child. That can be good or bad as an advocacy strategy.

If your team has already talked about this as a possibility, it's good to work together on the options. But they may also dig their heels in and take it personally as in, being offended because "We can meet his needs here, and I'm bothered that you think we can't." Weigh all of your options and think about possible scenarios as you proceed through this decision.

Advocacy Tip: I often have parents hire me so that they can get their child into a private placement. Oftentimes, early in the conversation, the parent will say something like, "I want to get him in XYZ private school because there everyone gets Orton-Gillingham (OG), JUMP Math, Responsive Classroom and The Writing Revolution."

Kudos to parents who know what programs will work for their kids, and there's nothing wrong with visualizing your child in a placement where they will thrive. But in situations like that, just work backward. If placement is based upon goals and services, start to build an IEP that points toward OG, JUMP Math, Responsive Classroom, and The Writing Revolution. What do those programs provide that your child needs? And why are the current interventions not working?

The IEP process doesn't change, sometimes you just need to work backward.

Least Restrictive Environment (LRE)

As I wrap up this chapter, you may notice that besides referencing it a few times, I have not discussed Least Restrictive Environment (LRE). LRE is a concept that entire books have been devoted to and entire workshops and conferences for educators and parents alike. For each of these IEP sections, I could do another hundred pages discussing all the ins and outs, but especially for LRE.

So, I'm going to try to be brief. First, the LRE is a continuum with a lot of placement options. The team is required to consider LRE when discussing placement. That does not mean that the student is required to try each step along the continuum, and there is nothing in IDEA that states this.

Second, a lot of people have a lot of opinions about LRE. How many times in this book have I said that you really need to dig in, learn something, and study it? This philosophy applies to LRE and inclusion, too. Read as much as you can. Watch videos, talk to parents, and most importantly talk with your children to the best of their ability about this. You know what works for your family and you will arrive at the right decision.

Your Play for This Chapter

Visit this section of your IEP. But think about what needs to change and how you are going to advocate for that change. A placement change is a big deal and will likely take more evaluations and several IEP meetings.

CHAPTER 19

Behavior Components of an IEP

Behavior-related questions far outnumber all the other individualized education program (IEP) questions I receive—combined. Parents have a child who is struggling with behavior challenges at school, and the school either isn't addressing it properly or things are getting worse.

If your child faces behavior challenges, you've likely heard terms like Functional Behavior Assessment (FBA) and Behavior Intervention Plan (BIP) tossed around. Maybe you've even heard terms like Behavior Improvement Plan or Positive Behavior Support Plan (PBSP). While the names vary, the principles remain the same, and understanding these tools is critical to advocating for your child.

This chapter will break down FBAs and BIPs, that is what they are, how they work, who writes and implements them, and what to do if the system isn't working. And because this is a big topic (and one of the most important), we'll dive deep into common issues, practical tips, and examples to help you navigate behavior challenges like a pro.

Why Are Behaviors Such a Big Deal?

Negative behaviors can have devastating consequences for our kids. Suspensions, expulsions, and even involvement with law enforcement are disproportionately common for children with disabilities. These aren't just "naughty behaviors." Often they're cries for help, rooted in unmet needs, trauma, or skill deficits.

For children with disabilities, behavior challenges are rarely about "acting out" for the sake of it. Many behaviors are the result of an inability to communicate, sensory overload, or an environment that doesn't accommodate their needs. Punitive approaches—like suspensions or detentions—don't address the root cause. Instead, they escalate the problem, often leading to a cycle of punishment and worsening behavior.

As a parent, it's overwhelming. You may feel like the school blames you or your child instead of addressing the underlying issues. Worse, poorly written FBAs and BIPs can compound the problem, focusing on superficial fixes instead of addressing root causes.

Let me say this upfront: I've become increasingly skeptical of FBAs. When I started out as an advocate, I frequently pushed for FBAs as a solution to behavior challenges. But now? I only recommend them as a last resort.

Why? Because in my experience, if the IEP is properly written and implemented with fidelity, many behavior challenges would never escalate to the point of requiring an FBA. So before diving into an FBA, make sure your child's IEP is rock-solid. Is their reading intervention appropriate? Are accommodations like sensory breaks or preferential seating being followed? Determining if your child's IEP meets all of their needs, and is being followed, is your starting point.

What Is a Functional Behavior Assessment (FBA)?

An FBA is like detective work for behavior. The goal is to figure out the function of the behavior: what's driving it and what the child is gaining or avoiding by engaging in it. Behaviors usually serve a purpose even if it's not immediately obvious.

The following are the key components of an FBA:

- **Defining the Behavior:** The team clearly describes the behavior in observable, measurable terms. For example, instead of saying "disruptive," they might define it as "leaving the classroom without permission more than three times per week."
- **Data Collection:** Observations and data are gathered to identify patterns. This includes looking at what happens before and after the behavior (the ABCs of behavior: Antecedent, Behavior, Consequence).
- **Hypothesis:** Based on the data, the team hypothesizes the function of the behavior. For example, is the child trying to avoid a task, meet a sensory need, or express frustration?
- **Recommendations:** The FBA concludes with recommendations for strategies and interventions to address the behavior's function.

While FBAs should ideally be conducted by someone with expertise in behavior analysis (like a Board-Certified Behavior Analyst or school psychologist), Individuals with Disabilities Education Act (IDEA) doesn't specify qualifications. This means anyone— from a teacher to a guidance counselor—can be tasked with conducting an FBA.

This is one of my biggest frustrations. Behavior analysis is a specialized skill, and when untrained individuals conduct FBAs, the results are often superficial or misguided.

What Is a Behavior Intervention Plan (BIP)?

A BIP is the action plan that comes out of the FBA. It outlines specific steps to address the behavior by teaching replacement behaviors and modifying the environment.

The following are the key components of a BIP:

- **Preventative Strategies:** Changes to the environment or routine to reduce triggers (e.g., offering movement breaks to prevent sensory overload)
- **Instruction in Lacking Skills:** Teaching skills the child is missing, like emotional regulation, communication, or task initiation
- **Replacement Behaviors:** Identifying appropriate alternatives to the problem behavior (e.g., asking for help instead of leaving the room)

- **Reinforcement Strategies:** Positive reinforcement for appropriate behaviors (e.g., praise, rewards, or extra playtime)
- **Consequences:** Clear, consistent responses to the behavior (e.g., calmly redirecting the child)
- **Data Collection:** Methods for tracking progress to ensure the plan is working

A BIP isn't just for the classroom teacher. It's for everyone who interacts with your child at school, including:

- General education and special education teachers
- Paraprofessionals and aides
- Support staff (e.g., bus drivers, cafeteria workers)

Consistency is critical. If everyone isn't on the same page, the plan won't work. And yes, I've seen many kids get suspended from the school bus due to behaviors on the bus.

Common Issues with FBAs and BIPs

Let's talk about what can go wrong and what you can do about it.

- **The Wrong Person Conducts the FBA**

  As mentioned earlier, FBAs are often conducted by staff without proper training. If your school assigns an inexperienced person, advocate for a qualified professional.
- **The IEP Isn't Being Implemented**

  Before agreeing to an FBA, ensure the existing IEP is being implemented as written. If accommodations or supports aren't being followed, that's likely contributing to the behavior.
- **Shallow Analysis**

  Many FBAs don't dig deep enough. For example, they might identify that a child avoids reading tasks but fail to address the underlying issue: the child can't read at grade level.
- **Blaming the Child**

  Too often, behavior plans focus solely on changing the child, without considering how the environment or teaching strategies could be improved.
- **Ignoring Trauma**

  Trauma is a significant factor in behavior, yet it's rarely addressed in FBAs or BIPs. If your child has experienced trauma, insist that it be considered in the analysis and plan.
- **Generic or Cookie-Cutter Plans**

  Many behavior plans are generic, offering strategies that don't align with the child's unique needs. For example, offering a sticker chart for a child with sensory needs won't address the underlying problem.

Finally, trauma-informed practices are often overlooked in schools. If your children have a history of trauma, it's crucial to incorporate this into their behavior plan. For example:

- Teach self-soothing techniques
- Provide a safe space for the child to de-escalate
- Train staff on how trauma affects behavior

Practical Tips for Effective Behavior Plans

Let's say a child frequently leaves the classroom when asked to complete writing tasks. A shallow FBA might conclude that the child is avoiding work and recommend consequences for leaving the room. A well-conducted FBA would dig deeper, revealing that the child has fine motor difficulties and experiences anxiety during writing tasks.

The resulting BIP might include:

- Teaching the child keyboarding skills as a replacement for handwriting.
- Providing breaks during writing tasks to reduce anxiety.
- Using positive reinforcement when the child completes a writing task.

As Dr. Ross Greene says, "Kids do well if they can." Behavior isn't random; it's communication. With the right supports, every child can succeed.

The following are practical tips for effective behavior plans:

- **Ask for Evidence-Based Strategies:** Ensure the plan includes proven methods for addressing behavior. Avoid buzzwords without substance.
- **Include Skill-Building:** Behavior plans should teach missing skills, not just manage symptoms.
- **Advocate for Positive Reinforcement:** Plans should focus on rewarding appropriate behavior rather than punishing negative behavior.
- **Monitor Progress:** Request regular updates and data to track whether the plan is working.
- **Stay Involved:** Your input as a parent is invaluable. If the plan isn't working, speak up and suggest adjustments.

Your Play for This Chapter

Take a deep dive into your child's FBA or BIP. Use the checklist included with this book to analyze whether it addresses the root causes of the behavior and includes the necessary supports. If it doesn't, it's time to advocate for changes.

PART 3

Advanced Game Planning

I have just explained more than a dozen major sections of an IEP. I hope as you went through each chapter, you paused to review your child's IEP, comparing it to what should ideally be in each section. Most parents who seek my services come to me with nothing more than a gut feeling that something is wrong with their IEP. They can't always articulate it, but they know something isn't working. My job is to help turn that gut feeling into actionable items. I hope the previous chapters have done that for you—section by section.

Knowing what a solid, meaningful IEP should look like, and your rights, is one thing. This section will provide ideas and strategies to make that happen for you.

Advanced
gRPC Features

CHAPTER 20

Choosing Your Next Play

So, now what? What do you do with all this information? What's the next step? I'm so glad you asked! You basically have five options moving forward.

Options for Moving Forward

Here are several paths you can take based on your situation. Whether your individualized education program (IEP) needs a complete overhaul or just some fine-tuning, there's a way forward.

Option 1: Do Nothing

Yes, this is technically an option. You can keep hobbling along year after year with an IEP that doesn't fully meet your child's needs. Maybe you're hoping the next teacher will be more accommodating or that the school will finally "get it" and create a solid IEP.

Here's the hard truth: I've never once seen this approach work. Not once. Schools don't miraculously decide to write a perfect IEP without input and advocacy from parents. So, if you choose this option, understand that you're relying on hope alone, which isn't a strategy.

Still, I get it. Sometimes, life gets overwhelming, and addressing IEP issues can feel like adding one more rock to an already overflowing backpack. If this is the option you choose for now, promise yourself it's temporary. Acknowledge the choice and set a time frame for when you'll revisit the issue.

For example: "I'm in the middle of a divorce right now, so I can't tackle this. But by the start of next school year, I'll make it a priority." Even naming a future date can help you feel less stuck.

Option 2: Prepare a Parent Concerns Letter for Your Next IEP Meeting

If your annual IEP meeting is coming up soon (within the next month or two), this is a solid option. A parent concerns letter is one of the most powerful tools in your advocacy toolbox.

It's your opportunity to put your concerns in writing, ensuring they become part of the official IEP process. I have more on this in Chapter 24.

Here's why this is important:

- Documentation is key. If your concerns aren't documented, they might as well not exist. A parent concerns letter becomes part of your child's educational record, creating a paper trail.
- A letter sets the agenda. When you send a concerns letter before the meeting, you're helping the team focus on the areas that matter most to your child.
- A letter clarifies your priorities. Schools are often juggling competing demands. Your letter ensures they know what you consider most urgent.

Here's what to include in your letter:

- A clear, concise list of your concerns. For example, "My child is not making progress in reading due to insufficient supports."
- Data or examples to back up your points. "On their last benchmark assessment, they scored at a first-grade level, despite being in third grade."
- Proposed solutions or questions. "Can we discuss adding a structured, evidence-based reading intervention like Orton-Gillingham (OG)?"

If your meeting isn't for several months, you might not want to wait that long to address serious issues. In that case, consider the next option.

Option 3: Do Nothing Now, But Make a Promise to Address It Later

Sometimes, life throws curveballs, and you simply don't have the bandwidth to tackle IEP issues right now. That's okay. You're human. But here's the deal: Don't let "later" turn into "never."

Write down your intention where you'll see it: a sticky note on your fridge, a reminder in your phone, or even a calendar appointment for a specific date.

For example:

- "By October 1, I'll schedule a meeting to address the lack of progress in math."
- "In January, after we settle into a new routine post-move, I'll revisit the issue of extended school year services."

Acknowledging that you need a break doesn't mean you're giving up. It just means you're prioritizing your family's overall well-being.

Option 4: Send an Email to Your IEP Team

For many parents, this will be the most practical and immediate option. After reviewing your IEP, you might have identified one or more areas that need improvement. Start by gathering your notes and formalizing them into an email. Not every concern needs to be addressed by an IEP meeting.

Examples of When You Should Request an IEP Meeting:

- If you've identified significant gaps or multiple issues, a meeting is likely necessary. For example: "I've noticed that several goals are vague, and there's no clear plan for how they'll be achieved. I'd like to request an IEP meeting to address these concerns."
- If you need to discuss adding services, accommodations, or supports.

Examples of When to Request a No-Meet Addendum:

- For smaller issues, you can request changes without a formal meeting. For example: "Can we update the Specially Designed Instruction (SDI) section to include access to noise-canceling headphones during tests?"

Tips for Writing the Email:

- Be clear and concise. Outline your concerns without overwhelming the team.
- Use a collaborative tone. Avoid accusations or emotional language. For example: "I'd like to work together to ensure that [child's name] has the support they need to succeed in math."
- Include a timeline. "If possible, I'd appreciate a response by [date]."

Option 5: Hire an Advocate or Attorney

Sometimes, despite your best efforts, the situation is too complex or contentious to handle alone. That's when it's time to bring in reinforcements. Advocates and attorneys are trained to navigate the IEP process and can provide invaluable support.

If you find yourself in any of these situations, you should consider hiring an advocate:

- If you're struggling to get your concerns taken seriously
- If the school is resistant to adding necessary services or accommodations
- If you feel overwhelmed by the process and need someone to guide you

If you find yourself in any of these situations, you should consider hiring an attorney:

- If your child's rights have been violated, e.g., being denied Free Appropriate Public Education (FAPE) or improperly disciplined

- If you're considering filing for due process
- If the relationship between you and the school has broken down completely

To find the right professional, look for someone experienced in special education law, ask for recommendations from other parents or local support groups, and then schedule a consultation to discuss your case and ensure they're a good fit.

Advocacy Tip

Once you've chosen your path, the key is to follow through. Advocacy isn't a one-time event: It's an ongoing process. Here's how to stay on top of things:

- **Keep a Paper Trail:** Document every interaction with the school, from emails to meeting notes. This isn't just about covering your bases; it also helps you track progress over time.
- **Stay Organized:** Use an IEP binder to keep all your child's records in one place. This will make it easier to find what you need when you need it.
- **Build Relationships:** Advocacy doesn't have to be adversarial. Whenever possible, approach the school team as collaborators. A positive working relationship can go a long way.
- **Educate Yourself:** The more you know about IDEA, state regulations, and best practices, the better equipped you'll be to advocate effectively. There are countless resources available, from books and webinars to parent support groups.
- **Celebrate Small Wins:** Advocacy can be exhausting, so don't forget to acknowledge progress along the way. Whether it's getting a single goal revised or securing a new service, every step forward matters.

The information in this book is powerful, but it's only useful if you act on it. Advocacy isn't easy, but it's one of the most important things you can do for your child. Remember, you're not just fighting for better grades or smoother school days; instead, you're fighting for your child's future.

Your Play for This Chapter

Choose one action item from this list and commit to it. Whether it's writing a parent concerns letter, scheduling an IEP meeting, or simply promising yourself to revisit the issue later, take that first step. Progress starts with action—and you've got this.

CHAPTER 21

Your IEP Meeting

IEP meetings: Parents hate them, schools hate them, everyone hates them. Just scroll through social media, and you'll see endless posts from parents venting, stressing, and sometimes even crying over them. Individualized education program (IEP) meetings are notorious for being contentious, adversarial, sad, and frustrating all at once. A whole rollercoaster of emotions crammed into one tiny room.

And let's be real: Some of that drama is inevitable. You've got a mix of parents advocating for their kids, school staff stretched thin, and a process that's complicated even on a good day. But here's where I need to give you a little finger wag (it's out of love, I promise). You don't have to let the stress of one meeting define your entire year. And you shouldn't.

The truth is, an IEP meeting is just one piece of the puzzle. Yes, it's important, but putting all your energy—and anxiety—into this one meeting is unnecessary. This brings me to a little secret, a game-changing mindset shift that I hope will give you an "aha!" moment. Ready? Here it is: The IEP meeting itself is *not* the most important part of the process. I know that might sound like heresy, but hear me out.

Why? Because the real work of an IEP happens outside that meeting. It's what you do *before* and *after* the meeting that makes the biggest difference for your child. Sure, what's said and done in the meeting matters, but it pales in comparison to what your documentation and paper trail say.

Let me give you an example. Those progress monitoring reports you get every quarter? Yeah, those. They're not just for show. Take them seriously. Carve out some time to read through them (no, not while you're half-watching Netflix). Really *read* them. Look for patterns. Compare what the school says your child is doing to what you see at home. And then—this is the key—*respond to them*. Let the school know you've received the report, share your observations, and ask for clarification if something doesn't add up.

And here's the beauty of it: You don't have to wait a whole year to make changes to your child's IEP. If something isn't working, request a meeting. Yes, you're allowed to do that. If a goal has been met or a strategy isn't effective, ask for updates. The Individuals with Disabilities Education Act (IDEA) doesn't say IEPs can only be touched once a year. The squeaky wheel gets the grease, my friends, but it has to squeak *in writing*.

Documentation is king. It's your shield, your sword, your whole arsenal when it comes to advocating for your child. And the good news? Anything can be documentation.

Homework that shows your child is struggling, an email exchange with a teacher, and a copy of a class newsletter where your child's name is missing can help paint a picture of your child's needs and progress.

Think about this: If your IEP meeting is full of condescending comments or dismissive attitudes from the team, what do you think that says about how the school views your child? If you're being gaslit or constantly told no, it's likely your child's needs aren't being met. But with a strong paper trail, you're not just relying on the team's words (or lack thereof). You have concrete evidence to back up your requests.

Still, let's not completely dismiss the meeting itself. It's important to be prepared. And preparation doesn't mean just skimming your IEP the night before or crossing your fingers that the team has done its homework. It means having a strategy. That's why I've put together an IEP Meeting Readiness Checklist (Appendix B): It's a lifesaver when you feel like you're juggling a thousand things.

Advocacy Tip: Always, always, always follow up the meeting with an email. Recap what was discussed in clear, bullet-point notes. This is critical for two reasons. First, it ensures that everyone is on the same page and that the final IEP you receive matches what was agreed upon. Second, it becomes part of your documentation. If something goes sideways later, you have a written record to fall back on.

In fact, treat IEP meetings as a business meeting. This is your job. You are in the business of getting your child's needs met. Look around the IEP table: Everyone else is being paid to be there except you. For them, this is a work meeting. It should be for you, too.

Let this business meeting mindset be the overarching approach to your planning. Would you walk into a business meeting at work unprepared? Then don't do it here either.

Would you wear torn sweatpants to a business meeting at work? Then why is it acceptable for *this* business meeting? I'm not suggesting you get a whole new wardrobe. A decent sweater or top and jeans is fine. Just not jeans torn to shreds with a super low cut top. It's just not professional.

I wish appearances didn't matter, but that's not the case. They do. If you want to be taken seriously, and you want your IEP team to care about your IEP more than one meeting a year, you need to do the same. Properly prepare; I have more resources for this at the back of this book.

Let's wrap this up with some real talk. Schools know which parents are engaged in the process and which ones aren't. If you're not actively participating, you're at risk of being overlooked or, worse, taken advantage of. The more you show that you're paying attention—reading every report, asking thoughtful questions, following up on details—the more seriously the team will take you. And more importantly, the more likely your children are to get the support they deserve.

So, yes, IEP meetings are stressful. But they don't have to be the overwhelming, end-all-be-all events we make them out to be. The real magic happens in the day-to-day work you do to advocate for your child, in the careful documentation you keep, and in the persistence you bring to the table. That's how you change the narrative, and that's how you make sure your child's needs are truly met.

Frequently Asked Questions (FAQs) about IEP Meetings

As an advocate, I've attended hundreds (maybe thousands?) of IEP meetings since 2009. While every child is different and there are countless scenarios that could happen in an IEP meeting, below are some of the more common questions I get about them.

- Who facilitates an IEP meeting? This varies by district and is not defined by IDEA. An ultimate goal is for students to eventually lead their own meetings.
- Who can request an IEP meeting? Any member of the IEP team may request a meeting.
- Whom should I bring to an IEP meeting? Parents should invite individuals with significant and relevant knowledge about the student. However, it's best to avoid bringing people like grandparents unless they understand the IEP process. Moral support is vital, but I've seen relatives who don't understand the process stress a parent out by being a distraction.
- Who can attend an IEP meeting? Anyone invited by an IEP team member who has relevant input about the child.
- Can an IEP meeting be held without a parent? In rare cases, yes. The district must make substantial efforts to involve the parent. Check your state regulations and IDEA's rules on parent participation.
- Can parents request an IEP meeting? Yes, parents have the right to request an IEP meeting whenever necessary.
- Can I record my IEP meeting? Yes, but follow your state's recording laws and check your school district website for policies. You may need to request in advance.
- What to expect in an IEP meeting? Some teams follow a formal agenda, while others go through the IEP section by section, making necessary updates.
- What happens in an IEP meeting? It's a collaborative review of the child's evaluations, progress, and IEP goals.
- Can an IEP meeting be postponed? Yes though districts often avoid this to remain compliant. Sometimes, delays are unavoidable.
- What is a facilitated IEP meeting? This involves an impartial facilitator guiding the meeting, often when discussions become contentious.
- Do gifted students have IEP meetings? This depends on your state. Check your Department of Education for guidance.
- Can we do the IEP meeting by phone? It's possible but not ideal. Face-to-face or virtual meetings are better for effective communication.
- How should an IEP meeting conclude? The next steps depend on the discussions and decisions made. Follow up with an after-meeting letter to confirm mutual understanding.
- What happens after an IEP meeting? Too often, parents disengage after the meeting. Instead, send an after-meeting letter to maintain momentum.

- Can we only do my IEP meeting in English? No. IDEA requires meetings to be conducted in the parent's native language.
- How long should an IEP meeting last? This varies based on the student's needs and the team's preparation.
- What is an initial IEP meeting? It's the first meeting after evaluations determine a need for an IEP. Be aware that initial attempts may need refinements.
- How do I request an IEP meeting? Always make your request in writing to either your child's teacher or case manager. If you do not have a designated person to communicate with, I'd email the person I communicate with most often, which is usually the teacher.
- What is an interim IEP meeting? This term is not officially defined in IDEA but generally refers to a meeting held before another one is scheduled to address additional needs.
- What is an emergency IEP meeting? Only two states recognize this concept. Check local guidelines for details.
- How often should an IEP meeting be held? IDEA requires an annual meeting at minimum.
- Can there be an IEP amendment without a meeting? Yes, not all changes require convening the full team.
- Who or what is the Local Education Agency (LEA) at an IEP meeting? The LEA representative ensures district compliance with IDEA and is able to make financial decisions on behalf of the district. In other words, the LEA is your school district. I don't know why IDEA couldn't just say "school district" but that's federal-speak for you!

Your Play for This Chapter

Look at the IEP meeting resources at the end of this book and make a mental note to use them when your meeting is pending.

CHAPTER 22

How to Prepare for an IEP Meeting

Preparing for an individualized education program (IEP) meeting can feel like gearing up for a major life event. And in some ways, it is. This isn't just another parent-teacher conference; it's a critical opportunity to advocate for your children and ensure they're getting what they need to succeed in school. The key to making the most of this meeting? Preparation. Lots of it.

This chapter is your guide to breaking down what might seem overwhelming into actionable steps, helping you walk into your IEP meeting confident, informed, and ready to advocate like a pro.

Understand the Purpose of the Meeting

Before diving into logistics, make sure you understand the purpose of the meeting. Is it your child's annual IEP review? A reevaluation meeting? Are you addressing specific concerns or adding new goals? Knowing the objective will guide your preparation and help you focus on what matters most.

Also, think about what *you* want to accomplish. Do you need to address areas where your child isn't making progress? Are you advocating for specific services, accommodations, or a change in placement? Keep these goals front and center as you prepare.

Sometimes, schools frame IEP meetings as a formality. Don't let that fool you. Every IEP meeting is an opportunity to advocate for your child's needs, update goals, and push for progress. It's your chance to ensure that what's written on paper matches what's happening in the classroom.

Collaborate with Your Child (If Appropriate)

If your children are old enough and it's developmentally appropriate, involve them in the process. After all, this is about *their* education. Ask how they feel about school, what's working, and what's not. You might be surprised by their insights.

For older students, the Individuals with Disabilities Education Act (IDEA) mandates that they be involved in transition planning by age 16 (or earlier in some states). Use this as an opportunity to empower them. Whether it's attending the meeting, preparing a statement, or simply sharing their thoughts with you beforehand, their voice matters.

For younger children, you can still include them in simple ways. Let them know that the meeting is about making school better for them. If they're comfortable, they can write a letter or draw a picture about what they like or dislike about school.

Participation can look different for every child. They might attend part of the meeting, prepare a video, or write a statement to be shared. The goal is to help them feel included without overwhelming them.

Gather and Organize Your Documents

Documentation is your secret weapon in IEP meetings. The more organized you are, the better positioned you'll be to advocate effectively. Here's what you'll want to have on hand:

- **Your Child's Current IEP:** Review it carefully. Highlight goals, services, accommodations, and notes about progress or lack thereof.
- **Progress Reports:** These provide valuable insight into whether your children are meeting their goals. Look for patterns and discrepancies.
- **Evaluations and Testing Data:** This includes both school-conducted assessments and any independent evaluations. They're the backbone of your case for services.
- **Communication Logs:** Keep copies of emails, notes, and letters to show a history of concerns and actions.
- **Homework Samples:** These can illustrate your child's struggles or progress.
- **Your Notes:** Write down anything you've observed at home, such as changes in behavior, strengths, or challenges.

Use a binder or digital system to keep everything organized. If you're using my IEP Meeting Checklist, you're already ahead of the game.

Know Your Rights

Understanding your rights under IDEA is crucial. You don't have to memorize the entire Procedural Safeguards document (let's be real, it's a slog), but you should know the basics:

- You can request an IEP meeting at any time if you feel it's necessary.
- You have the right to participate as an equal member of the team.
- You can bring anyone with you, including an advocate, friend, or family member, as long as the school is notified.
- You're not obligated to sign anything on the spot. If you need time to think, take it.

Knowing your rights gives you the confidence to speak up and push back if needed. It also prevents you from being steamrolled by school staff who might (intentionally or unintentionally) misrepresent what's possible or required.

Prepare Your Questions and Requests

Take some time to brainstorm what you want to ask or address during the meeting. Write these down—you'll thank yourself later when your mind goes blank during a heated discussion.

Here are some questions to get you started:

- Are the current goals appropriate and challenging enough?
- Are accommodations being implemented consistently?
- What data are being used to measure progress?
- Are additional services or supports needed?

If you're making specific requests, back them up with data. For example, if you're asking for occupational therapy (OT), bring evaluations or notes that support the need. The more evidence you have, the harder it is for the team to say no.

Anticipate Challenges

Let's be real: Not every IEP meeting is smooth sailing. School teams might push back, argue against your requests, or even deny that there's a problem. This is where preparation pays off.

Think ahead about potential objections. If you're asking for a costly service, for instance, be ready to counter arguments like "We don't have the budget." Bring data and documentation to show why the service is necessary.

And remember, you don't have to agree to everything during the meeting. If you feel pressured or unsure, ask to reconvene later. The IEP process is a marathon, not a sprint.

Bring an Advocate or Support Person

You don't have to do this alone. An advocate, friend, or family member can provide emotional support, take notes, or help you push back if the team isn't being cooperative.

Advocates, in particular, can be a game-changer. They understand the process, know the law, and can speak up when emotions run high. Even if the meeting isn't contentious, having someone in your corner can make a huge difference.

Use My IEP Meeting Note-Taking Template

During the meeting, it's easy to lose track of what's being said. My IEP Meeting Notes Template helps you stay organized and ensures you don't miss any key points.

After the meeting, compare your notes to the final IEP document. If something doesn't match, address it immediately.

Plan Your Follow-Up Email

Once the meeting is over, send a follow-up email summarizing what was discussed, as discussed in the previous chapter. This creates a written record and ensures everyone is on the same page.

Keep it concise and to the point:

- The meeting date and attendees
- Key topics discussed
- Decisions made
- Next steps and deadlines

If there were any discrepancies or issues, now's the time to document them.

Take Care of Yourself

IEP meetings can be emotionally draining. It's okay to feel overwhelmed, and just means you care deeply about your child.

Get a good night's sleep beforehand, eat something before the meeting, and practice deep breathing if you're anxious. Remember, you're doing an amazing job by showing up and advocating for your child.

If the meeting doesn't go as planned, don't lose hope. The IEP process is ongoing, and there's always an opportunity to revisit and revise.

IEP meetings aren't just a one-and-done event; instead, they're a cornerstone of your children's education. The more prepared you are, the more effectively you can advocate for their needs. And when in doubt, remember: you're not alone. This is a journey, but with the right preparation, you've got everything you need to make it a successful one.

Your Play for this Chapter

Use tools like my IEP Meeting Checklist and Notes Template to stay organized and focused. They're at the back of this book.

CHAPTER 23

Tips for Writing to Your IEP Team

I f I could offer one golden rule for navigating the individualized education program (IEP) process, it would be this: Document everything.

What you say to IEP team members during meetings or phone calls matters, but unless it's in writing, it didn't happen. In IEP disputes, everything comes down to documentation. That's why it's crucial to follow up verbal conversations with written communication, ideally via email.

Why email? It's perfectly appropriate (and legal!) for handling IEP matters. It provides a time- and date-stamped record of your interactions, which can be invaluable if issues arise later. Whether you're clarifying a conversation, asking for a follow-up, or expressing concerns, email ensures there's a paper trail to support your advocacy.

Eight Essential Tips for Writing to Your IEP Team

Let's break this down into actionable steps with tips to help you communicate effectively and professionally with your child's IEP team.

Tip #1: Be Clear and Concise

Stick to the facts, and don't bury your main point in a wall of text.

- State your purpose right away. Start your email with a clear statement of why you're writing. For example: "I'm writing to follow up on our discussion during the IEP meeting on [date]."
- Avoid rambling or including unnecessary details. If your email is too long or unfocused, the team may overlook critical points.

Tip #2: Use a Professional Tone

Even if you're frustrated, keep your communication respectful.

- Avoid accusatory or emotional language. Instead of writing, "Mrs. Teacher didn't do her job," reframe it to focus on your child: "My child did not receive his XYZ service for two weeks."
- Think of your email as a document that could be read by a neutral third party, like a mediator or hearing officer. Keep it professional.

Tip #3: Create a Paper Trail

Documenting everything is non-negotiable.

- After verbal conversations, send a follow-up email summarizing what was discussed. For example: "Thank you for speaking with me today about [topic]. As we discussed, [recap of the main points]. Please let me know if I've missed or misunderstood anything."
- Keep copies of all emails, letters, and responses in your IEP binder or digital folder.

Tip #4: Focus on Your Child

Always center your message on your child's needs.

- Avoid personal attacks or making it about the teacher's or school's shortcomings. For example, don't say, "You're failing my child." Instead, say, "My child isn't making progress on his reading goal as outlined in the IEP. What additional supports can we implement to address this?"
- Use specific examples to highlight concerns. For instance: "During the past two weeks, my child has brought home incomplete assignments because he was unable to finish during class. How can we support them in completing their work?"

Tip #5: Don't CC the Entire World

Resist the urge to copy every person in the district on your email.

- Start with the chain of command. Address your email to the teacher or case manager first.
- If you don't receive a response within a reasonable timeframe (usually two to three business days), escalate to the next level, such as the principal or special education director.

Tip #6: Ask Direct Questions

If you need clarification or action, phrase your questions clearly.

- Example: "Can you confirm if the sensory breaks outlined in the IEP are being implemented during [specific times]?"
- Avoid vague statements like, "I don't think the IEP is being followed." Instead, be specific: "The IEP states that my child will receive speech therapy twice a week, but I see from the service log that this has only happened once in the past month. Can you explain why this is happening?"

Tip #7: Set a Collaborative Tone

Advocacy doesn't have to mean conflict. Start and end your emails on a positive note while remaining firm about your concerns.

- Open with gratitude or an acknowledgment of effort. For example: "Thank you for all the work you're doing to support my child this year."
- Close with a cooperative statement, such as: "I look forward to working together to ensure [child's name] has the support they need to succeed."

Tip #8: Be Patient and Set Timelines

Follow up appropriately, but give the team time to respond.

- End your email with a clear timeframe: "If I do not hear from you by [specific date], I will follow up again."
- Avoid sending multiple emails in rapid succession. Give the team a chance to address your concerns.

Why Documentation Matters

Here's the hard truth: If it's not in writing, it might as well not have happened.

Imagine you end up in a due process hearing. Without documentation, it becomes a game of "he said, she said." On the other hand, if you have a clear, written record of your interactions with the school, you're in a much stronger position.

That's why I always say: Dance like no one is watching, but email like it might be subpoenaed someday.

Examples of Good Communication

As a one-to-one advocate for families, I write a lot of my clients' communication. And I read and proofread a lot of their communication. The errors fall into two categories: Either they were too brief, or they over-thought it and rambled on for too long. Aim for the middle, meaning be careful and professional in your communication and take your time. But don't overthink it and write something too long.

Here are some templates to get you started.

Example 1: Following Up After a Meeting

Subject: Follow-Up: IEP Meeting on [Date]

Dear [Case Manager's Name],

Thank you for meeting with me today to discuss [child's name]'s IEP. I want to confirm my understanding of what we discussed:

1. [Recap main point 1]
2. [Recap main point 2]
3. [Recap main point 3]

Please let me know if I've misunderstood or left anything out. I look forward to seeing the revised IEP by [specific date].

Sincerely,
[Your Name]

Example 2: Requesting Action

Subject: Request for Clarification on IEP Implementation

Dear [Teacher/Case Manager's Name],

I've noticed that [child's name] has been struggling with [specific issue]. According to the IEP, [specific service or accommodation] should be provided to address this. Can you confirm if this is being implemented? If not, I'd like to schedule a meeting to discuss next steps.

Thank you for your time and support.

Sincerely,
[Your Name]

Effective communication is one of the most powerful tools you have as a parent. By documenting everything and using a clear, professional tone, you can advocate for your child while building a collaborative relationship with the IEP team.

FAQs about IEPs and Email

When IDEA 1975 was passed, email was not a thing. In fact, it still wasn't a thing when IDEA was reauthorized in 1990. The times change, but legislation and guidance catch up. Email is a practical and legal method of communication between you and your IEP team.

Can a school use email to send out IEPs and related information? Yes. It just makes good business sense. It's fast, it's easy, and it is accepted practice. However, if a parent does not have a computer and/or email, all of the information must be presented to in a format that can be accessed.

Can I "virtually" sign the IEP documents and return them via email? The Office of Special Education Programs (OSEP) has issued guidance about this issue. But again, it has to be accessible to the parent.

Can school staff use personal email to handle IEP issues? It is not best practice, but it is not illegal either. This is an issue that would most likely be handled by Personnel/HR as it likely violates school employment policies. But it is not against the law or addressed in IDEA.

The school told me that I can only email one person! This is also a very common practice, not just in schools but in many workplaces. Putting a parent on an IEP communication plan is acceptable and it has been upheld with case law. It makes sense to have communication flow through one person. It prevents redundancy, confusion, and other issues. Do not take offense if you have been asked to only communicate with one person on the team. IEP Staff often have very large caseloads and this increases efficiency.

Can the school put me on a "communication plan?" Yes. The Office of Civil Rights has ruled in many complaint decisions that putting a parent on a communication plan does not deny FAPE to the child. (A communication plan is when the school asks you to only email one person, one day a week or something like that.) Except for extreme situations, there really shouldn't be a reason to be continually emailing all the team members.

How long does the school have to respond to my email? This is not something defined by IDEA in most states. Generally, common courtesy is to allow three to five days before I start pestering for a response. It's important to know your state regulations.

When should I send the IEP team an email? You can use it for just about anything. Email is a great way to build your data and paper trail for concerns that you have and supports that you are requesting.

Can I make official requests over email? Absolutely! And you should. It time stamps exactly when you made the request.

Your goal is simple: Ensure your child gets the support they need. And with these tips, you'll be well-equipped to do just that.

Your Play for This Chapter

If you have a specific email you need to write to your IEP team, do that. Otherwise, a simple organizing tip for better advocacy: Whatever email provider you use, create a sorting folder called "IEP." Yeah, not terribly clever. But get used to putting every email from the school in that folder. Even if it doesn't feel like, in that moment, it is related to IEP. It might be needed as data and documentation later, and you'll be glad you have it.

CHAPTER 24

Writing an Effective Parent Concerns Letter

Writing to your individualized education program (IEP) team is pretty common, so why is this chapter in the "Advanced Game Planning" part of the book? It's because writing a solid Parent Concerns Letter that gets results is an advanced play. Most parents write to their IEP team often—sometimes too often.

I read these emails because clients share them with me. And they're chock full of mistakes, feelings instead of data, and worse. There is a difference between "writing to your IEP team" and "writing to your IEP team and getting positive action as a result."

This is one of the most underutilized portions of the IEP process: the Parent Concerns Letter.

It is YOUR right to submit one and have your letter, in its entirety, included in the IEP. As a parent, it is also your duty to your children: This is their time, their voice, their opportunity to be heard in the IEP.

What Is an IEP Parent Concerns Letter?

An IEP Parent Concerns Letter is your chance to speak up about anything that's been bothering you regarding your child's IEP. Think of it as putting your thoughts on paper so the school team knows exactly what's on your mind and what your child needs.

Here's what it usually includes:

- **What are Your IEP Concerns:** Start by laying out your concerns. Maybe your child isn't making the progress you expected, or you're noticing some behaviors that worry you. Whatever it is, this is your space to say, "Hey, something's not right here."

- **What You're Seeing:** Back up your concerns with observations or data. Share what you've noticed at home, in child's homework, or even in conversations with teachers. If reports from the school aren't matching what you know about your child, mention it.

- **What You Want to Happen:** Be clear about what you're asking for. Do you need more evaluations? A tweak in the IEP goals? Maybe some extra support or a meeting to hash things out? Spell it out.
- **Keep It to Just Facts:** This letter becomes part of your child's IEP file, so keep it respectful and to the point. It's your written record that says, "I'm involved, and here's what I think needs to happen."

Think of it as your way to ensure the school team is on the same page as you. Plus, having everything in writing can be invaluable if your IEP situation becomes contentious in the future.

Where Is the Parent Concerns Letter Mentioned in IDEA?

Great question! IDEA doesn't explicitly call out a "Parent Concerns Letter." However, it emphasizes parent participation numerous times. And when Individuals with Disabilities Education Act (IDEA) is reauthorized, the committee sends out a lengthy explanation, essentially a "What we mean by this" guide.

For example, on page 140 of the guidance addendum, it underscores the importance of parent input:

> *"The IEP process must ensure that the parents' concerns for enhancing the education of their child are considered...."*

So, while the law may not specify a "Parent Concerns Letter," your role and input as a parent are foundational to the IEP process.

If you're told that your letter does not have to be included in the IEP, that is a huge red flag that the IEP team does not respect your parental rights. If you are told this, a quick, "Hmm, that's not my understanding. Can you show me where it says that in IDEA?" Hint: The team won't be able to find it.

If it persists, consider a compliance complaint. This information is in your procedural safeguards.

How Long Can the Parent Concerns Letter Be?

As long as it needs to be. If a school claims it must be 200 words or fewer, they're likely limited by their computer program, not the law. They'll need a workaround to include your full input.

That said, aim for clarity and conciseness. Don't send a 37-page manifesto; instead, focus on what's critical. Be detailed but reasonable.

To provide even more context and detail, you could include sections like "Academic History," "Observations from Home," or "Specific Strategies that Work." These can offer additional clarity and depth to your concerns without overwhelming the team.

When Do I Send the Parent Concerns Letter?

There are two main times to write and send this letter:

1. **Before the Annual IEP Meeting:** When you RSVP to the meeting, include your letter. For example:

   "Yes, I can attend. Here is my list of IEP parent concerns that I wish to discuss."
2. **When You Have Concerns:** If you're requesting a meeting, evaluations, or changes to the IEP, include your letter with your request.

The key is to ensure your concerns are documented and included in the IEP. By documenting concerns before the meeting, you help the team prepare and ensure that discussions are more productive and focused.

Additional Tips for a Strong Parent Concerns Letter

Here are five ways to make your letter even more impactful:

1. **Use Specific Examples:**
   - Instead of saying, "My child struggles with math," say, "My child is having difficulty with multiplication and word problems as shown by their recent test scores (45% on the last assessment) and struggles with homework."
2. **Include Data:**
   - Reference progress reports, report cards, or even anecdotal evidence like "My child spends 90 minutes on a single worksheet and often ends up in tears."
3. **Focus on Solutions:**
   - Frame your concerns around what can help. For example: "Given the challenges in reading fluency, I'd like to request additional support in the form of one-on-one reading interventions or assistive technology."
4. **Stay Child-Focused:**
   - Avoid placing blame on the school or staff. Instead, focus on how the current situation impacts your child: "The frequent changes in staffing have made it difficult for my child to build trust and consistency, which affects his ability to stay engaged."

5. **Set Goals:**

   - Include measurable outcomes you'd like to see. For example: "By the end of the quarter, I'd like my child to achieve a reading fluency score of at least 85 words per minute."

IEP Parent Input Statement Examples

Here's what you might include:

Academic Concerns:

- "My child struggles with reading comprehension, especially with longer texts. Let's explore strategies to break down complex material."
- "Math continues to be a challenge, particularly word problems. He needs clear goals to address this."

Behavioral/Social Concerns:

- "My child struggles with managing frustration, leading to outbursts. A behavior plan would help."
- "He feels isolated at school. Social skills training or peer mentoring could make a difference."

Emotional/Well-being Concerns:

- "Anxiety during transitions impacts his learning. Accommodations for smoother transitions are essential."
- "School refusal has increased due to anxiety. Let's find ways to reduce this stress."

Strengths and Interests:

- "His excel in technology. Can we incorporate more tech-based learning?"
- "Art is calming for him. Let's explore ways to integrate art into his day."

Communication Needs:

- "He benefit from visual supports and clear instructions. Let's include this in his routine."
- "Extra processing time helps him participate fully."

Sending Your Parent Concerns Letter

Once you've gathered all that you wish to include, it's time to hit "send." Or is it? Remember, this will become a part of your child's educational record, so keep it professional and sleep on it before sending.

1. Type it Up: Send it via email and follow up with a signed hard copy.

2. Be Transparent: Let them know you expect it to be included in the IEP. For example: "I'm sending this electronically so it can be copied into the Parent Concerns section of the IEP."

3. Avoid Surprises: Don't drop major requests at the meeting. If you have the data to back up a big request (a one-to-one aide or private placement, for example), step out of that comfort zone, be assertive, and ask for it in your letter. There is an advocacy philosophy out there, that if you surprise the team at the meeting, it won't have time to fully prepare its "no." This is misguided at best. When is an IEP team ever afraid to say no to a parent?

4. Use a Bullet-Point or numbered List: This format is easier to follow and track during meetings.

5. Get in the habit of eliminating words from your correspondence that are weak. For example: I just, I think, I feel, I wish, I would like to suggest, If, Possibly.

6. Use instead: I am requesting, He is, He has, I am asking for.

7. Weak Language Example: I would like to request an IEP meeting because I think we need to discuss possible placement changes. Stronger: I am requesting an IEP team meeting to discuss "name" placement change and what that would look like once implemented. Notice I said, "once implemented." I didn't say "if implemented."

8. Grammarly is a free Chrome extension. Use it or use some similar application.

9. Write it then sleep on it. Never send a letter immediately after writing it. It is very likely you'll have a few more things to add or subtract. I understand the sense of urgency in fixing IEP issues, but temper that and make it one really good letter. And that can take a few days to a few weeks.

10. Get a friend or spouse to proofread and offer an opinion. Or you're welcome to post it on my message boards for feedback (**https://forums.adayinourshoes.com**).

11. State each issue only once but give several examples under each concern. Example: "Ethan is struggling to keep track of his assignments and homework. He has Executive Functioning deficits. (List examples of missing assignments, homework, etc.) But then that's it for the EF issues, got it? Keep it as succinct as possible while getting your concerns documented.

12. I recommend two to three examples for each concern. Try to have examples that cross environments, such as classroom, bus, home, cafeteria, after school activities. This will show that the issue is occurring in many environments but is the same issue. Remember: Each issue/concern once with two to three examples.

13. Use Action Words. Examples are am, is, does, has, exhibits, struggles, works, maintains.

14. I am writing to you about my child's "name," who is a student in your building and has Mrs. ABC for homeroom (if writing to the principal-my son's elementary school has 1,600 students, I don't expect him to remember every detail). I am requesting an IEP placement change from his current placement to XYZ.

15. Use power words: I am requesting. Not "I would like to request...." Power words.

Sample Template

"Dear IEP Team Leader,

I'm looking forward to our upcoming IEP meeting. Here are the parent concerns I wish to discuss:

- Concern 1
- Concern 2

Thank you for ensuring these are included in the Parent Concerns section of the IEP."

Parent Input Forms

Some schools provide a parent input form. Yes, fill it out. But *also* submit your Parent Concerns Letter. Forms can be limiting, and you're not restricted to just using theirs. Your concerns must still be included in the IEP even if you've filled out their form

Once you have written your letter, you have to proofread and edit it. And once you see the list below, I bet you will have some changes to make.

It's important that your language in their form is professional and cordial. The Parent Concerns Letter or a Parental Input form is your chance to shape your child's education. It ensures your voice is part of the process and provides a written record of your involvement. Don't underestimate its power. It's not just a letter; it's advocacy in action. Take the time to write it well and make it count for your child's future.

Your Play for This Chapter

Write a Parent Concerns Letter if you need to.

CHAPTER 25

Understanding Prior Written Notice (PWN)

One of the most important parental rights in this process is also one of the most misunderstood. Welcome to Prior Written Notice or PWN. Pennsylvanians, we call it the NOREP. As far as I know, we're the only state that has a different name for it, but I could be wrong.

Firstly, parents get hung up on the word "prior" so let me clear that up before we move on. Prior in Prior Written Notice means prior to the action taking place. It does not mean prior to the individualized education program (IEP) meeting. It does not mean that an IEP team members cannot blindside you at an IEP meeting, which happens all the time.

It means that they have to provide written notice before they actually do the thing they just blindsided you with.

PWN is a very clunky term. And, it's in the Parental Rights/Procedural Safeguards booklet that most IEP parents never even read. You should receive an annual copy of your Procedural Safeguards. The school usually gives them to you at your annual IEP meeting or as part of the evaluation process.

Parents before us fought and lobbied for this addition to IDEA when it was reauthorized.

What Is Prior Written Notice?

Under the Individuals with Disabilities Education Act (IDEA), Prior Written Notice is a formal written communication that schools must provide to parents whenever they:

1. Propose to initiate or change the identification, evaluation, or educational placement of a child or the provision of a Free Appropriate Public Education (FAPE).
2. Refuse to initiate or change those things.

Simply put, it's the school's way of saying, "Hey, here's what we're doing (or not doing) and why." And this isn't just a polite suggestion. It's required by law.

Why Should You Care About PWN?

Here's why this document is a game changer:

- **Transparency:** PWN forces the school to lay its cards on the table. They must explain *why* they're making a decision, along with the evidence and reasoning behind it.
- **Accountability:** It creates a written record. This is crucial for tracking decisions over time and ensuring that your child's rights are protected.
- **Advocacy Tool:** A clear PWN can highlight gaps or inconsistencies in the school's approach, which you can address to better advocate for your child.

What Does a Proper PWN Include?

According to IDEA, a PWN must include:

1. A description of the action the school is proposing **or refusing to take**.
2. An explanation of why the school is proposing or refusing the action.
3. A description of the evaluation, records, or reports used as the basis for the decision.
4. A statement of your rights, including how you can obtain procedural safeguards.
5. Sources for assistance, such as contact information for your state's Parent Training and Information Center.
6. Other options considered and why they were rejected.
7. Other relevant factors affecting the decision.

I hope with the bolded text in point one, that a few lightbulbs are going off. Now do you see why it is so important to have a solid Parent Concerns Letter written? Because if the school is going to refuse to take the action you suggested, it must provide you with a PWN stating this. And that has to include why it is denying it, what else it considered, and what data it used to make this decision.

In my extensive experience, I find that when an IEP team is in a meeting and the members all surrounded by their coworkers, it's very easy to give a verbal no. It's much more difficult for them to say no in writing, especially in response to a well written letter supported with progress monitoring data. I could go on all day about it, and in fact in my online training Don't IEP Alone Academy, I spend three or four sessions just on understanding this with step-by-step instructions how to pair a parent concerns letter with the PWN as an essential and effective advocacy tool.

The "Wait and See"

The concept of "wait and see" is one I see frequently in IEP meetings, and nothing is ever 100%, as a general rule I advise my clients to never agree to the "wait and see." Wait and see has a few cousins: the "why don't we try" or "how about for now, we...."

Because "wait and see" and all of its cousins are just a friendlier, less confrontational way of saying no. You've just been told "no" but it may not feel like it. And when this happens, parents may not push for the PWN because they don't feel fully rejected.

An example: Your child is struggling with reading and so the team put him in a Tier 1 Multi-Tiered System of Supports (MTSS) class for support. Half the school year has gone by and you don't think enough progress has been made. You've done your research and it appears that an Orton-Gillingham (OG) program for 90 minutes a day, could really close the reading ability gap between your child and his peers. So, you ask for it.

But at the meeting, the team suggests that instead of the OG program you asked for, it wants to move him to a Tier 2 MTSS program instead. You discuss it for a little while, and at some point, someone on the team says, "Well, why don't we try the Tier 2 intervention for a while?"

That doesn't really sound like a no, does it? It gives hope to the parent that their suggestion will be implemented at some point. But, in my professional experience, that day never comes without significant advocacy. The team often hopes you will forget about this or not bring it up again. And since it doesn't feel like a no, parents may not push the issue on a PWN if they even know what a PWN is and does. The Local Education Agency (LEA) will often issue a PWN without this on it, because after all, technically they never said no or "refused to implement" as the guidelines for PWN state.

I have witnessed this same scenario many times with parents asking for a Functional Behavior Assessment (FBA), asking for a different placement, asking for more or different services. "Wait and see" is just a softer-landing no.

If it's out of your comfort zone to push back on this right now, at least put a timeline on that wait and see. Using the above scenario, a reply might be, "Sure, let's try the Tier 2 intervention for eight more weeks. If Jacob has not improved his reading ability by ABC and XYZ by that time, I'll make a request for the team to reconvene and further discuss an OG program for him."

Rather than my absolute advice of "never agree to the wait and see," I should rephrase it to "never agree to an open-ended wait and see."

Real-World Examples of PWN in Action

Here are some situations when a parent should expect to receive a PWN.

When You Request Evaluations

Imagine you notice your child struggling with reading comprehension. You request a comprehensive evaluation for dyslexia. The school must respond with a PWN, either agreeing to conduct the evaluation or explaining why it doesn't think it's necessary. Its response must outline the specific reasons for the decision and the data it's relying on.

When Services Are Changed

Your child receives occupational therapy twice a week, but suddenly, the school proposes cutting it to once a week due to staffing issues. You receive a PWN stating the proposal, the justification (e.g., staffing shortages), and the data supporting its belief that this reduction won't impact your child's progress. If this reasoning doesn't sit well with you, the PWN becomes your starting point to challenge the decision.

When Placements Are Denied

You request that your child transition from a self-contained classroom to an inclusion setting. The school denies the request, citing concerns about your child's ability to manage in a less structured environment. The PWN must include the data supporting the school's decision—perhaps behavioral records or teacher observations—and any options it considered, such as additional supports within the inclusion setting.

How to Use PWN to Your Advantage

Parents and advocates before us fought hard to get the PWN written into IDEA revisions and updates. Prior to the PWN being a part of parents' rights, schools could change IEPs without notifying parents.

1. Request It in Writing. If you disagree with a school's decision or need clarity, formally request a PWN. This puts the burden on the school to articulate its reasoning.

    Sample Request: *"I am requesting Prior Written Notice regarding the decision to deny [specific service/request] for [child's name]. Please include the data and reasoning used to make this determination."*
2. Analyze It. When you receive a PWN, ask yourself:
    • Does it address the required elements (action, reasoning, evidence, options, etc.)?
    • Are the school's justifications backed by solid data or evaluations?
    • Does the reasoning make sense, or are there gaps or inconsistencies?
3. Use It as a Springboard for Action. A detailed PWN can guide your next steps:
    • If the school cites data you haven't seen, request copies.
    • If the reasoning seems flawed, ask clarifying questions.
    • If you spot a procedural misstep, you may have grounds for a state complaint or due process hearing.

Red Flags in PWN (and What to Do About Them)

Just because it's required doesn't mean that every school does a stellar job at completing PWN Forms.

• Vague Explanations: If the school says, "We're denying the request because it's not needed," push back. Ask the school to provide specific data and explain the rationale.

- Lack of Data: If the PWN doesn't reference evaluations, observations, or other evidence, request the underlying documentation.
- Failure to Address All Options: Schools must consider a range of options and explain why they chose one over another. If this isn't clear, ask them to elaborate.

Empower Yourself: How to Request a Better PWN

Sometimes, the PWN you receive is incomplete or confusing. Here's how to fix that:

1. Ask Specific Questions: If a PWN is vague, follow up in writing. For example:
   - *"Can you clarify what data were used to justify this decision?"*
   - *"What alternative placements were considered, and why were they rejected?"*
2. Request Supporting Documents: If the PWN mentions evaluations or reports, ask for copies. This allows you to cross-check the reasoning against the actual data.
3. Document Everything: If you notice discrepancies between what's happening in practice and what's outlined in the PWN, write it down. These notes can be critical if you need to escalate.

This is one of those times where, if being assertive doesn't come naturally to you, you're going to have to take a deep breath and just do it. Otherwise, if a school denies you something and gives a weak PWN as a follow-up that you don't challenge, you've just told it that you won't exercise your rights. Schools know what a PWN is and the power it holds, which is why they sometimes don't issue them or issue incomplete ones.

You've just left the door wide open for being taken advantage of. And that's why this is an advanced play because parents all over the country ignore this very important right every day.

Your Play for This Chapter

At every IEP meeting, you should receive a copy of your Parents' Rights, or Procedural Safeguards. Make a plan to read them, especially the part about the PWN. I say "make a plan" because the booklet is long and it's dry reading. If you do not have a copy, you can do an Internet search for "your state + IEP procedural safeguards" to find an online copy.

CHAPTER 26

IEP Progress Monitoring

I t's one of the most important parts of the individualized education program (IEP) process, and yet it's the topic that I get the fewest questions about. I think the concept is just so overwhelming and confusing that parents don't know what to ask. They just have that gut feeling that their child isn't progressing.

But IEPs are not driven by gut feelings. We have to back it up with data.

Let's revisit sports again. The goals are your end zones, the services and accommodations are your team's plays, and progress monitoring is your scoreboard. Without that scoreboard, you're running plays without knowing if you're winning or even advancing the ball.

Unfortunately, schools don't always make it clear what the score is, leaving many parents feeling like they're playing in the dark. But don't worry: By the end of this chapter, you'll know exactly how to track progress and keep your team on the path to victory.

Okay, this is where many districts fail to see the big picture. From a parent's perspective, it's easy to determine why you would want to monitor your children's progress toward their IEP goals.

But this is important for districts as well!

School districts can get important information to use, such as:

- assess student outcomes
- submit mandated state and federal reports
- claim Medicaid reimbursements in many states
- help identify and support requests for additional staffing needs
- identify professional development gaps
- guide the district's Specially Designed Instruction (SDI) strategies
- make decisions about student growth
- communicate progress on IEP goals, evaluations, and placement
- determine the effectiveness of providers, programs, and curricula

What is IEP progress monitoring? Why is progress monitoring toward IEP goals needed? Who is responsible for each IEP goal? How do you progress monitor IEP goals? Are there any IEP progress monitoring tools? Most parents look at the goals and know in their gut that their child isn't making progress. But they are not sure of what to do about IEP progress monitoring.

IDEA states that each child's IEP must contain the following:

(3) A description of—

i. How the child's progress toward meeting the annual goals described in paragraph (2) of this section will be measured; and
ii. When periodic reports on the progress the child is making toward meeting the annual goals (such as through the use of quarterly or other periodic reports, concurrent with the issuance of report cards) will be provided. . . [§300.320(a)(3)]

What Should an IEP Progress Report Look Like?

Let's start with the basics. What does a progress report even look like? By law, schools must report on your children's progress toward their IEP goals at least as often as other students receive report cards. That means quarterly or trimester updates, depending on the school calendar.

A proper progress report should include:

- Specific data related to each goal: This could be percentages, frequency counts, or other measurable criteria.
- Comparison to the baseline: Where did your children start at the beginning of the year? This helps you see if they're growing.
- Clear alignment with the goals: The report should directly address the goals written in the IEP, not just general "Johnny is doing fine" statements.

IEP Progress Monitoring *has to be* more than just test scores. Copying a test score from an evaluation, such as a standard score of 76 on Written Expression, will not tell you about that child's strengths and weaknesses.

Nor will it tell you how the specific skill area impacts a child's ability in the general education curriculum. Achievement evaluations will also not be able to be repeated at regular intervals for monitoring.

Decide where you want to start and where you want to end up: the baseline and the goal. For every goal, you want to ask the IEP team:

- How will progress be measured? Are these data objective?
- Who will measure the progress?
- What will be reported to parents?
- How often or when will progress be measured?

The same IEP progress monitoring process should be used for the length of the goal:

- Can this assessment or procedure be repeated at specific intervals?
- Were these data just from an observation?
- Was a checklist or rubric used to reduce the influence of personal feelings, inconsistency, and the possibility of bias in the process?

An IEP should pass a stranger test, and that includes IEP goals. If a child moves or a new teacher takes over a class, will that teacher be able to measure the progress in the same way?

Is there a Curriculum-Based Measurement (CBM) that can measure this progress objectively? Will work samples, checklists, rubrics, and assessment data be shared with you?

How Often Should You Receive Progress Monitoring Reports?

As shown above, Individuals with Disabilities Education Act (IDEA) says "concurrent with the issuance or report cards...". It's worth noting that IDEA does not say "only with report cards." You can advocate for more frequent progress monitoring, especially in critical areas. If the school has reported significant behavior or learning disability needs, it may not be appropriate to wait nine weeks to know if the child is progressing.

If parents don't address progress monitoring during the IEP meeting while the IEP is being developed, they likely will be very disappointed when progress reports are issued.

Bonus Advocacy Tip: I often run into pushback from IEP teams when my clients ask for more frequent progress monitoring. But here's the thing. The school personnel isn't only collecting IEP data three or four times a year. They should be collecting it year-round. We're not asking for "more" when we ask for more frequent reports. After all, they're doing this anyway. We're just asking that it be shared with us more frequently. Sometimes, that reminder that this isn't going to be more work for them is the nudge they need.

Because if you have a fifth grader reading at a first-grade level, why in the world would you wait to see if the reading strategies are working?

Common Issues with Progress Reports

Here's what progress reports shouldn't be:

- Vague: If the report says "making progress" without any data, that's a red flag.
- Non-specific: Statements like "improving in math" tell you nothing about how your child is meeting their IEP goal of solving two-step equations.

- Confusing: If it takes a Ph.D. to interpret the data, the school isn't doing its job. Again, ask for help if you need it.
- Opinions and subjective data are often not accurate. Observations without checklists or rubrics are often not accurate.
- Grades are not objective assessments of progress because many factors can influence grades.
- Be careful of non-specific goals such as "Johnny will write at fourth grade level standards." You want a goal to explain what the fourth grade standard is, so the expected action is clear to everyone.
- Another red flag to look for is that goals or data that aren't measurable. Guessing a mood, feeling, or attitude cannot be measurable. A statement such as "Jacob's executive functioning skills have really improved since Christmas" does not tell us much. Specific examples would include how many fewer assignments or books he's lost or how many assignments he was able to finish without prompting.
- Another red flag is when an IEP Goal does not have baseline data. You must know where the children currently is in their performance or achievement to be realistic about where you want them to end up.

Pro Tip: If you've received one of these "fluffy" reports, request clarification in writing. Ask for specific data points, comparisons to the baseline, and details about what has been achieved toward each goal.

How to Interpret Progress Data

Progress data can come in many forms, including:

- Percentages (e.g., "Johnny answers 80% of comprehension questions correctly.")
- Frequency counts (e.g., "Uses coping strategies five times per day.")
- Rubrics or Checklists (e.g., "Meets criteria in three out of five trials.")

Here's how to decode the numbers:

1. Compare to the Baseline: Look at where your child started. If the goal was to increase correct responses from 50% to 80% and the current report says 70%, you're on track.
2. Check the Goal Deadline: If your child is halfway through the school year and the goal deadline is June, is the progress where it should be?
3. Ask Questions: If something doesn't make sense, email the team. "The progress report says Johnny is using coping skills three times a week, but the goal was five times daily. Can we review these data?"

Remember how many times I've now said to ask for help interpreting those evaluation reports if you need it? If you don't know what the evaluations mean, how are you going to know if your child is making progress or not? Because the "eye test" may work in sports, but it doesn't work here.

For you non-sports fans, the "eye test" in sports refers to evaluating a player or team based on observation rather than using statistics, analytics, or other data-driven measures. Essentially, it's about what you see when watching the game—how a player moves, their skill level, decision-making, effort, and overall performance—without relying on numbers to back up the assessment.

What to Do If Progress Is Stalling

If your child isn't making progress, don't panic, but don't wait. Here's your action plan:

1. Request a Meeting: You can call an IEP meeting anytime if there's a concern. Send an email formally requesting it.
2. Bring Data: Review the reports, gather your own observations, and bring any outside evaluations.
3. Propose Adjustments: This might mean tweaking the goal, changing the services, or adding supports like assistive technology.
4. Document Everything: Keep all communication in writing and save every report, email, and draft. This paper trail is your best friend.

Tracking Progress at Home

Sometimes, school reports don't match what you're seeing at home. Sound familiar? You can track your child's progress yourself using tools like:

- Checklists: For goals related to daily living skills or behavior.
- Home Data Logs: Record instances of specific behaviors or skills.
- Apps: There are apps to track behavior, academic milestones, and even therapy progress.

Progress monitoring isn't just a box to check; it's how you ensure your children get what they need. Yes, it's exhausting to stay on top of this, but your persistence matters. None of us asked to be on this team, but here we are, right? I never wanted to become an expert in my son's educational data, but his success depends on it.

Remember, schools have limited resources, and the loudest advocates often get the most attention. Stay loud, stay organized, and don't settle for vague answers.

Your child's success is worth it.

Your Play for This Chapter

Surely, by now, you know that I'm going to direct you to your child's IEP progress monitoring data, and start to learn it.

CHAPTER 27

Common Parent Mistakes in the IEP process

When you know the common individualized education program (IEP) mistakes, you can steer clear of them and save yourself a ton of frustration.

These strategies will help you feel more grounded and take some of the anxiety out of the process. Understanding the process means you're not just being heard; instead, you're being *listened to*. When that happens, barriers start coming down, and suddenly, you're getting to *Yes* in a system that loves to say *No*.

And trust me: When that shift happens, those IEP meetings won't feel quite so daunting.

Before I share a list of common parent IEP mistakes, I want to address one big one. I call it, the "gotcha!" And "gotcha!" is not an effective advocacy strategy. It's a parent mistake because it only serves to make your relationship with your IEP worse, not more collaborative.

Gotcha is a slang term for "I have got you." While I haven't actually ever heard parents yell that term out loud to school staff (thank goodness!), in this situation it usually happens internally. According to Cambridge Dictionary, the definition is said to mean "I have got you" in order to surprise or frighten someone you have caught, ***or to show that you have an advantage over them*** (bold mine).

This is a typical example of what happens during a "gotcha" moment in an IEP situation. Parents uncover clear proof that the school has made a mistake and feel like this evidence will finally give them some leverage during IEP negotiations. Most likely, the parents are thinking they can use this misstep to gain an upper hand with the IEP team. The assumption is that catching the school in an error will leave them scrambling to make amends and grant every request in the next meeting.

But here's the truth: It doesn't work like that. When you walk into a meeting and your focus is criticizing the team, no matter how much evidence you have, it's not going to be a collaborative meeting. It's not. If you have a crappy district or crappy IEP team, you have a crappy IEP team. Even when presented with mountains of evidence, crappy IEP teams do not admit that they are wrong.

That's not to say we let teams off the hook when they make mistakes that matter. I would just recommend that you are more intentional with how you handle it rather than hoping for that big "gotcha!" at the IEP meeting. Learn how to get supports and services added to your IEP because you have an overwhelming amount of data and documentation, not a gotcha.

Focus on what we can control and the cards we've been dealt. The IEP process is not fair and balanced. Schools have more resources, and you will be outnumbered at IEP meetings. You have parental rights so, learn them and use them instead of a gotcha.

Thirteen Common IEP Mistakes Parents Make (and How to Avoid Them)

1. Not Getting Everything in Writing.

   If it's not written down, it didn't happen. Always follow up verbal conversations with an email:

   "Dear Mrs. Special Ed Teacher, thanks for chatting with me today. I wanted to summarize our conversation to ensure we're on the same page."

   Include a bullet-point list of key points. I once spoke to a mom who verbally requested evaluations four times in six months. Because there was no written documentation, the school acted as if those requests never happened. Every conversation must have a paper trail.

2. Underestimating Your Role as an Equal Team Member.

   You are just as important as anyone else on the IEP team. Fancy titles, degrees, and ties don't give school staff a monopoly on decision making. You know your child better than anyone else. Don't let intimidation keep you from advocating effectively. Your voice matters just as much—if not more.

3. Ignoring the Parental Concerns section of the IEP.

   This section is your opportunity to ensure your concerns are documented. Always come to meetings with a list of issues you want addressed. When you RSVP to the meeting invitation, send your list ahead of time.

   "Here's a list of parental concerns I'd like to discuss at the IEP meeting."

   By law, the team must address every concern you raise on a Prior Written Notice (PWN).

4. Being Too Polite or Forgiving.

   Niceness is great, but don't let it stop you from demanding what your child needs. If the right staff members aren't at the meeting, don't proceed. If the meeting ends before addressing all concerns, insist on reconvening. Don't let time slots or convenience dictate what's best for your child. If the dentist only cleaned your top teeth and told you to come back later for the bottom, you wouldn't just leave, right? Same applies here. Stop being so nice, so forgiving. Speak up. This is your time to discuss the needs of your child. In the real world, things don't fit into nice packages and time slots. I am not going to sacrifice my child's education for an administrative inconvenience.

5. Blindly Requesting More Services.

   More isn't always better. What matters is the right amount of the right services. For example, asking for more speech therapy won't help if a hearing issue is being overlooked. All the Occupational Therapy (OT) in the world to practice fine motor and handwriting doesn't matter if the OT isn't addressing unnoticed dysgraphia. Focus on evaluations to pinpoint specific needs before throwing solutions at the wall to see what sticks.

6. Accepting a "Rubber-Stamp" IEP Process.

   Don't let the school rush you through a pre-written IEP. If the meeting feels like a formality, it probably is. Push for meaningful collaboration. This is about your child's education, not fitting into someone else's schedule. Your time—and your child's future—are worth the extra effort. I call it the Jiffy Lube IEP Meeting, meaning in and out in 45 minutes. You go in, they read the IEP to you, there's minimal discussion, and you're on your way.

7. Comparing IEPs.

   IEPs are just that: *individualized*. What works for one child might not be appropriate for yours. Avoid arguments like, *"I want my child to have PT twice a week like the Smiths."* Focus on what your child needs, not what others are getting.

8. Losing Focus on the Child.

   It's easy to let emotions about past conflicts with staff creep into meetings. Don't let grievances distract you from the goal: getting what your child needs. Save disputes for other avenues, like formal complaints or discussions with administrators. Keep the focus on your child, always.

9. Overlooking the Importance of Data.

   Your child's IEP should be driven by measurable data. If goals aren't supported by frequent, relevant data, the process becomes guesswork. Don't accept vague progress reports. Ask for consistent, objective, and comparable data over time. If the school can't provide it, insist on changes.

10. Failing to Push Back Against Bias.

    Schools often default to viewing behaviors as defiance rather than a result of underlying needs, such as sensory issues or anxiety. Don't accept punitive responses without first addressing root causes. Advocate for supports that reduce triggers, not just consequences for the behavior.

11. Ignoring Self-Advocacy.

    As children grow, teaching them to advocate for themselves becomes essential. Help them understand their accommodations and how to communicate their needs to teachers. This can make a significant difference as they transition into adulthood.

12. Underestimating the Power of Questions.

    If something doesn't make sense—ask! Whether it's about evaluations, accommodations, or progress reports, don't hesitate to seek clarification. Schools often rely on jargon that can feel confusing. Demystify it by asking direct questions.

13. Not Taking Time to Reflect.

   After each meeting, take time to review the IEP and notes. Did the team address all your concerns? Are the goals actionable? Reflection ensures nothing slips through the cracks. Did you do a follow up email after the meeting?

Avoiding these mistakes won't just make the process smoother; it'll help ensure your child gets the education and support they deserve.

Your Play for This Chapter

Reflect on this list and think about what you can improve. How are you going to improve on the mistakes you're making, and what is your timeline for yourself?

CHAPTER 28

Independent Education Evaluations

What Is an Independent Educational Evaluation (IEE)?

One time, I was on a conference call with some other advocates, and we were working on developing a program just for kids who share my child's same diagnosis. At one point, one of them said, "Just tell them to go get an IEE."

I couldn't help myself from interrupting. Because here's the thing: a parent requests an IEE and the school says no, the school is required by law to file for Due Process! This is in Individuals with Disabilities Education Act (IDEA).

Most parents don't know this about IEEs. Couple this with the urban legend of "Every child has the right to an IEE" which is not true, and it's a recipe for disaster. The true statement is "Every child has the right to an IEE, subject to specific conditions...." The exact words in IDEA are "...subject to paragraphs (b) through (e) of this section."

I'm not going to copy and paste all of those paragraphs. Because I am going to give an overview. All that to say, this is why I consider asking for an independent education evaluation not a move for beginners. You must know the criteria and circumstances for one and have an action plan of what you're going to do if the school says no and files for Due Process as IDEA requires.

Because I can tell you how this plays out for most parents who don't understand this. They ask for an IEE, thinking they'll get one. The school says no, and when it sends that decision out to the parents, there is a Prior Written Notice (PWN) stating that the school has filed for Due Process. Most parents are shocked and overwhelmed by this, so they withdraw their IEE request. You don't want to be blindsided by this, so here's a plan of what to do next.

In the simplest terms, an IEE is a second opinion. It's an evaluation of your child's educational, behavioral, or developmental needs conducted by a qualified professional who isn't employed by the school district. The goal of an IEE is to provide a fresh perspective, often in cases where parents disagree with the school's evaluation or feel that additional insights are needed.

Think of it this way: If your doctor gave you a treatment plan that didn't sit right with you, you'd get a second opinion. An IEE works the same way but in the context of your child's education.

When Might a Parent Request an IEE?

There are several situations where you might decide it's time to request an IEE:

- The district does not employ qualified evaluators to conduct a specific evaluation.
- You disagree with the results of the district's evaluation.
- The district's evaluation was incomplete or relied on outdated methods or data.
- The data collected during the evaluation were inappropriate. For example, the district may have used a test protocol that is not suitable for a child with autism, intellectual disabilities (IDD), non-verbal communication, blindness, or reading disabilities.

What if the school says no?
Ah, the dreaded "No." What happens if you request an IEE, and the school pushes back?

1. It Must Provide a PWN.

    By law, the school must issue a PWN explaining why they're denying your request. This document should include their reasons and any supporting information.
2. IDEA requires the school to file for Due Process to defend its evaluations.

    If the school refuses your request, it has two options:
    - Agree to fund the IEE.
    - Prove in a Due Process hearing that its evaluation is appropriate.
3. You Can Fund the IEE Yourself.

    If the school successfully defends its evaluation in Due Process or simply refuses to pay, you can choose to fund the IEE privately. In some cases, if you later prove that the school's evaluation was inadequate, you can seek reimbursement.

Criteria for Warranting an IEE

Not every disagreement automatically means an IEE is necessary. Here are some situations where requesting one makes sense:

- Inadequate Assessments: The school didn't evaluate all areas of suspected disability (e.g., it tested for reading but ignored writing).
- Questionable Methodology: The evaluation used outdated tools or didn't follow best practices.
- Conflicts of Interest: You suspect the evaluator may have been biased or under pressure to minimize findings. This may be difficult to prove on paper.
- Insufficient Expertise: Your child's needs require a specialist (e.g., a neuropsychologist for complex neurological issues).
- Significant Discrepancies: There's a big gap between what the school reported and what you observe.

Types of IEEs and What Happens During Them

There are many kinds of IEEs, each tailored to different areas of need. Let's break it down:

1. Neuropsychological Evaluation:
   - Purpose: Identifies learning disabilities, ADHD, autism, and other cognitive or developmental conditions.
   - What Happens: A neuropsychologist conducts a series of tests to assess memory, attention, executive functioning, and processing speed. The evaluation often includes academic testing and observations.

2. Speech and Language Evaluation:
   - Purpose: Evaluates speech articulation, language comprehension, expressive language, and social communication.
   - What Happens: A speech-language pathologist (SLP) assesses your child's ability to understand and produce language, both verbally and nonverbally.

3. Occupational Therapy (OT) Evaluation:
   - Purpose: Examines fine motor skills, sensory processing, and activities of daily living (e.g., writing, self-care).
   - What Happens: The OT uses tools and activities to measure how your child processes sensory input and performs tasks requiring coordination.

4. Functional Behavioral Assessment (FBA):
   - Purpose: Identifies the root causes of challenging behaviors and develops strategies to address them.
   - What Happens: A behavior specialist observes your child in various settings and collects data to create a Behavior Intervention Plan (BIP).

5. Psychoeducational Evaluation:
   - Purpose: Assesses academic skills, cognitive abilities, and emotional functioning.
   - What Happens: This type of evaluation includes IQ testing, academic achievement tests, and assessments of social-emotional health.

6. Assistive Technology (AT) Evaluation:
   - Purpose: Determines whether your children need technology tools to access their education.
   - What Happens: The evaluator identifies and trials devices (e.g., communication devices, apps, adaptive keyboards) to see what best supports your children.

7. Independent Observations:
   - Purpose: Provides insight into how your child functions in specific environments (e.g., the classroom).
   - What Happens: An evaluator observes your child in real-time, looking for triggers, supports, and other factors affecting their performance.

How to Request an IEE

Earlier in the book, when talking about requesting IEP evaluations, I advised you to list what you are seeing, to be very specific, and give specific examples.

Now I'm reversing course because the context is reversed. Now the burden is on the school district to prove that its evaluation is appropriate. Remember, the school district has to file for Due Process if they say no. So, do you really want to show all your cards here? Do you want the team to know the parts of their evaluation process that you find fault with? You may want to meet with an attorney before you make your request the lawyer will have to develop a legal strategy if the school says no.

Another consideration is this, which I've seen happen numerous times: The parent requested an IEE. The school didn't say no, but brought the parent in for a meeting to discuss the request. Instead of saying yes or no to the IEE, it offered the parent a new set of evaluations done by the school. As an advocate, this feels a lot like "wait and see" to me. You may feel differently. During that meeting however, should you find yourself in this situation, my advice would be to not commit. A simple, "Well, let me think about this for a day or two and get back to you" is what I recommend.

One more important point for parents to know: You only get one time (one IEE) per issue. For example, you disagree with the school's evaluations because you think your child is dyslexic. The school personnel approves an IEE, and the independent evaluator agrees that your child is not dyslexic. That's it: You get one play for an IEE for dyslexia. You can't ask for another and another, hoping that an evaluator will find dyslexia.

That demonstrates why the IEE process needs to be well thought out and well planned for. You must research all the evaluators in your area and know which ones specialize in your child's suspected disability. The school is required to provide you a list of evaluators, but you do not have to choose from that list. Also, the school cannot put a price amount on an IEE. If either of those things happen, I suggest calling your state's Department of Education hotline (most states have them) and asking for clarification.

Whomever you speak with on the phone, ask the person to follow up by sending you an email or ask where you can reference this official policy online. Always best to have data and documentation; remember, people do not like to be told that they are wrong!

What Happens After the IEE?

Once the IEE is completed, you'll receive a detailed report with the evaluator's findings and recommendations. Then what?

1. Review the Report Thoroughly.

    Take time to understand the results. If there's jargon or findings you don't understand, don't hesitate to ask the evaluator or another professional to explain.
2. Share the Report with the School.

    Provide a copy to the school and request an IEP meeting to discuss the findings. The school is required to consider the results but isn't obligated to implement every recommendation.

3. Advocate for Implementation.

   Use the IEE as a tool to push for appropriate services and supports. If the school resists, refer to the evaluator's recommendations and insist it provide data to justify any refusals.

4. Incorporate New Goals and Supports.

   The IEE often leads to updated IEP goals, accommodations, or services. Be prepared to discuss how these changes will be implemented and monitored.

5. Keep It for the Long Haul.

   The IEE report can be a valuable resource for years to come, especially if your child's needs evolve or you need to advocate for them in new settings.

Over the years, I have had many clients who had neuropsychological evaluations. When done well, a "neuropsych" (the slang term) is a wonderful thing to have. Most parents, upon reading their child's neuropsych report, felt like it was the first time someone truly "got" their child.

I have never had any of my clients ask for an IEE and then receive that PWN stating that the district has filed for Due Process. Presumably, this is because the district knows that the parent has an advocate, and that the parent can prove on paper that the IEE is warranted.

I have, however, over the years, received many panicked and frantic phone calls from parents who did ask for an IEE, did receive the notice that the district filed for Due Process, and were blindsided and wanted to hire me to fix the situation. Whenever Due Process is on the horizon, I send parents to attorneys. I live in a litigious part of the country and would be doing my clients an incredible disservice by helping them with Due Process. All of the school districts around me have large legal firms on retainer whose attorneys spend all day, every day, doing things like this. It's naive to think I can do this.

In some states, advocates routinely help clients with Due Process. How you proceed is up to you, but my professional recommendation is to at least do an initial consult with a special education attorney. Many parents assume they cannot afford one, but you don't know for sure until you ask.

Side note: Make sure that the attorney is a special education attorney. Not a civil rights or family attorney, or a "Well, I usually do divorce, but I can help you." IDEA is a very niche area of practice.

Why IEEs Matter

IEEs bring specialized expertise, objectivity, and credibility to the table, helping you ensure your children get the support they need. The reason that school districts work so hard to deny them is because they know that an IEE report will often list many previously unidentified areas of need. And IEE reports come with a list of targeted interventions and supports that will work for the child.

Remember that paper trail and data and documentation that I've been browbeating you about for this entire book? An IEE can be the big missing piece of data or documentation that your child needs. Still, not every child needs an IEE nor should every parent ask for one. Here in suburban Philadelphia, a neuropsych (which is just one type of IEE) costs in the ballpark of $5,000–$8,000. So, schools shouldn't hand them out to whoever asks for one.

Requesting an IEE can feel like a bold move, but sometimes it's the necessary bold moves that make the biggest difference. The big takeaway I want you to get from this chapter is this: An IEE can be the missing piece you need to get your children what they need. But how you get there needs to thought about carefully, with your strategy planned out.

There's no real play for this chapter because it'd be disingenuous of me to say, "Go look at your IEP and decide if you need an IEE." If you think your child needs one, you're going to do that anyway. So, my play is to ask you to make a mental note or promise to yourself that if you disagree with your child's next set of evaluations, you will come back to this chapter.

CHAPTER 29

The Handoff: Next Steps in Advocacy

Well, you did it. You read and learned all the different parts of an individualized education program (IEP). You read how to compose an effective Parent Concerns Letter and prepare for an IEP meeting. Now you might be ready to take your advocacy even further.

Effective advocacy for your child isn't just fixing one IEP or attending one IEP meeting. It's an ongoing process that will need your attention for their entire school career. Even when things are fine with your children, their IEP, and their progress, it's important to keep good records and documentation of what is working, so it doesn't get removed when your children make progress.

I have an assortment of advocacy tools, templates, and ideas for you to use. You can find them on my website at **https://adayinourshoes.com/playbook**, and I've also provided several of them in the appendices. These are some of the tools and letters that I use when I am working one-on-one with clients.

In addition, I have a free message board at: **https://village.adayinourshoes.com** where parents can ask their personal IEP and 504 questions. Not every IEP question or concern needs to be on social media, or maybe you're not on social media. My message boards are private, you can remain anonymous, and I have several professional advocates who answer questions. Yes, every question is answered by a professional advocate!

When you go to the resources online, you can learn more about my online advocacy training, mini courses and more.

How to Become a Special Education Advocate

I want to thank you again for allowing me to be a small part of this big journey. Most professional advocates, myself included, started out just like you. We got a diagnosis and were drafted to a team we didn't want to be on.

But many parents like doing this. I know, sounds crazy! When you're struggling to even get through your own child's IEP meeting, attending IEP meetings for a living sounds nuts! I didn't want to be drafted to this team, but it turns out that I'm IEP MVP material.

I'll leave you with a few tips and ideas for those considering special education advocacy as a career. Trust me, no shortage of clients!

This is my list of what you need to become a Special Education Advocate.

- **Training:** While many advocates are "self-taught," the best ones prioritize ongoing training. There is no required certification or licensing to become a Special Education Advocate, nor is there a nationally recognized certifying body. However, attending training programs is invaluable for building your knowledge base and skills.

- **Experience:** Knowledge is essential, but hands-on experience is where you'll learn the most. Volunteering with agencies, becoming an Individuals with Disabilities Education Act (IDEA) Educational Surrogate, or assisting friends and family are great ways to start. Each case you handle will deepen your understanding and broaden your expertise.

- **Building a Business:** Once you've established yourself as an advocate, it's time to decide on your career path. Will you work independently, or do you prefer to join an agency? If you're starting your own business, you'll need a plan. How will you set your rates? Bill clients? Manage your workload? (Psst... I cover all of this in my online training!)

- **Writing Skills:** Advocacy is heavily reliant on documentation. If you've ever heard the phrase, "It's all about the paper trail," you'll understand why writing is a crucial skill. From drafting correspondence to creating detailed records, you'll need to communicate clearly and effectively.

- **Research Skills:** No two children are the same, and no two cases will be either. A solid training program is helpful, but a great advocate knows where to find reliable information when new challenges arise. Sometimes, the answers are buried in obscure regulations or case law, so staying resourceful and adaptable is key.

- **People Skills:** This job is as much about relationships as it is about laws and policies. You'll often find yourself resolving conflicts and working to rebuild trust between parents and schools. Your goals are not only to meet the child's needs but also to help repair strained relationships so families can continue working with their schools long-term.

- **Patience and Optimism:** This field can test your endurance. From egos to bureaucracy, it takes patience to navigate the challenges. Advocates are often called when things go wrong, not to celebrate successes. Staying optimistic and focusing on the positives—no matter how small—can keep you grounded and motivated.

Becoming a Special Education Advocate isn't just about mastering laws or procedures. It's about committing to the families you serve, navigating complex systems, and making a meaningful difference for kids.

But I love it, and I hope that at least a few people who read this book love it, too. Feel free to reach out if you have questions about becoming an advocate. There's also plenty of information on my sites (**adayinourshoes.com** and **dontiepalone.com**).

And now it's time for the handoff. Or the ball is in your court. Whichever works for you.

APPENDIXES

Practice Drills

In the appendixes, you'll find an assortment of tools and templates and ideas for you to use in your advocacy. These are some of the tools and letters that I use when I am working one-on-one with clients. You can also find these forms on my website (**https://adayinourshoes.com/playbook**).

APPENDIXES

Practice Drills

Appendix A: Glossary of Special Education Terms and Acronyms

This appendix contains a glossary of commonly used terms in special education, along with definitions. It also contains a list of 100 acronyms.

504 Plan A plan under Section 504 that provides accommodations for students with disabilities who do not qualify for an IEP.

2004 IDEA Refers to the most recent reauthorization of the Individuals with Disabilities Education Act, which clarified and expanded the rights of students with disabilities and their families.

ABA Applied Behavior Analysis: A therapeutic approach that uses reinforcement strategies to improve behavior and skills, commonly used with students on the autism spectrum.

Accommodations Changes that allow a person with a disability to participate fully in an activity. Examples include extended time, different test format, and alterations to a classroom.

ADA Americans with Disabilities Act: A civil rights law that prohibits discrimination against individuals with disabilities in all areas of public life, including schools.

ADD Attention Deficit Disorder: An outdated term now included under ADHD, describing difficulties with attention and focus.

ADHD Attention Deficit Hyperactivity Disorder: A neurodevelopmental disorder characterized by inattention, hyperactivity, and impulsivity.

Admission, Review and Dismissal (ARD) In some states, the name given to the committee (in other states not using the term ARD, they are called IEP teams or IEP committees) that is responsible for the development and review of a child's individualized education plan (IEP), evaluation and re-evaluation, Functional Behavior Analysis (FBA), and Behavior Intervention Plan (BIP). The ARD committee meets at least once per year to review the IEP and construct a new plan for the coming year. As far as I know, Texas is the only state that uses this term.

Antecedent Behavioral Consequences Chart (ABC) A tool used to create a record of disruptive behaviors that is utilized as part of Functional Behavior Analysis (FBA) to help to determine the triggers of and motivations behind these behaviors. ABCs are used to record what happened just before a behavior, a description of the behavior itself, and the consequence of the behavior.

APE   Adapted Physical Education: A physical education program tailored to meet the needs of students with disabilities.

Applied Behavior Analysis (ABA)   A technique for correcting behavior and social skill deficits in children with special needs. It is based on the understanding that children are more likely to repeat desired behaviors when these behaviors are met with positive reinforcement, and they are less likely to repeat undesirable behaviors that are not rewarded. One significant part of ABA is Discrete Trial Training (DTT), in which a skill is broken down into its most basic components so these components may be taught one at a time.

Assistive Technology (AT)   Assistive technology is technology used by individuals with disabilities in order to perform functions that might otherwise be difficult or impossible. AT can include mobility devices, such as walkers and wheelchairs as well as hardware, software, and peripherals that assist people with disabilities in accessing computers or other information technologies.

Augmentative and Alternative Communication Device (AAC)   AAC includes all forms of communication (other than oral speech) that are used to express thoughts, needs, wants, and ideas. An AAC device is a tool that uses a non-speech mode of communication to augment spoken language. AAC devices include electronic devices that digitize or synthesize speech and non-electronic communication aids such as manual communication boards.

Collaborative Teaching   A teaching strategy in which two or more teachers work together, sharing responsibilities to help all students succeed in the classroom. Also known as co-taught classrooms.

Curriculum-Based Measurements (CBM)   Small, regular evaluations used to determine how well a student is learning in various subject areas. CBM can involve checklists or oral questions, which the teacher uses to gauge student understanding and skill in a particular curriculum. These measurements are part of the monitoring component of the Response to Intervention (RTI) process.

Data-Based Decisions   A component of the RTI process that involves using information collected through the screening process to determine the intensity and duration of the needed intervention. NOTE: RTI and Multi-Tiered System of Supports (MTSS) are General Education (GEN ED) programs, not special ed.

DB   Deaf-Blindness: A dual sensory impairment affecting both vision and hearing that significantly impacts communication and learning.

DIBELS   Dynamic Indicators of Basic Early Literacy Skills: A set of assessments used to monitor the development of early reading skills.

DTT   Discrete Trial Training: A structured teaching method used in ABA therapy that breaks skills into small, manageable steps.

Due Process   Special education term used to describe the process where parents may disagree with the program recommendations of the school district.

ED   Emotional Disturbance: An IDEA disability category for students with significant emotional or mental health challenges.

EI   Early Intervention: Services provided to children from birth to age three to address developmental delays.

ESY   Extended School Year: Special education services provided beyond the standard school year to prevent skill regression.

FAPE   Free Appropriate Public Education: A legal right under IDEA that guarantees students with disabilities access to tailored education services at no cost to families.

FBA   Functional Behavior Assessment: An evaluation used to determine the causes and functions of a student's challenging behaviors.

FERPA   Family Educational Rights and Privacy Act: A federal law protecting the privacy of student education records.

IDEA   Individuals with Disabilities Education Act: A federal law that ensures services to children with disabilities.

IEE   Independent Educational Evaluation: An evaluation conducted by a qualified examiner outside of the school system, often at the school's expense.

Independent Educational Evaluation (IEE)   If the parent disagrees with the results of a school district's evaluation conducted on their child, they have the right to request an IEE. The district must provide parents with information about how to obtain an IEE. An IEE means an evaluation conducted by a qualified examiner who is not employed by the school district. Public expense means the school district pays for the full cost of the evaluation and it is provided at no cost to the parent.

Individualized Family Service Plan: (IFSP)   A process of providing early intervention services for children ages 0–3 with special needs. Family based needs are identified and a written plan is developed and reviewed periodically.

Individualized Transition Plan (ITP)   This plan starts at age 16/14/12 (depending on your state) and addresses areas of post-school activities, post-secondary education, employment, community experiences, and daily living skills.

Informed Consent   The signed consent of a parent that describes what the parent is consenting to; informed consent must be obtained before a district assesses, makes a major revision to a child's program, continues, or stops service for a child's disability.

Intellectual Disability (ID)   Significantly subaverage general intellectual functioning, existing simultaneously with deficits in adaptive behavior and manifested during the developmental period that adversely affects a child's educational performance. ID has been referred to as "Mental Retardation" (MR) in the past, and the term and its acronym may be used colloquially or on older documentation. (The federal government has passed legislation changing this term, but the legislation gave the states no deadline for changing the term in state laws/documents. Most states have already changed the term.) It is not, however, a currently accepted practice to refer to individuals with IDs as mentally retarded.

Interventions   Sets of teaching procedures used by educators to help students who are struggling with a skill or lesson succeed in the classroom.

IQ   Intelligence Quotient: A measure of cognitive ability often used in evaluations to determine eligibility for special education.

LD   Learning Disability: A disorder in one or more basic psychological processes involved in understanding or using language, such as dyslexia or dyscalculia.

Least Restrictive Environment (LRE)   The placement of a special needs student in a manner promoting the maximum possible interaction with the general school population. Placement options are offered on a continuum including regular classroom with no support services, regular classroom with support services, designated instruction services, special day classes, and private special education programs.

Local Education Agency (LEA)   Term used to describe a school district.

MD   Multiple Disabilities: An IDEA category for students with two or more disabilities that create complex educational needs; sometimes called MDS for multiple disabilities support.

MTSS   Multi-Tiered System of Supports: A framework for providing targeted academic and behavioral support to all students, often involving a Response to Intervention (RTI).

OHI   Other Health Impairment: An IDEA category for students whose health issues, such as ADHD or epilepsy, limit their strength, energy, or alertness.

OI   Orthopedic Impairment: A disability involving physical impairments that affect a student's ability to access education.

OSEP   Office of Special Education Programs: A federal agency that oversees IDEA implementation.

PBIS   Positive Behavioral Interventions and Supports: A proactive approach to improving student behavior through reinforcement and data-driven strategies.

PLAAFP   Present Levels of Academic Achievement and Functional Performance: A required section of the IEP that describes the student's current abilities and challenges.

PLOP   Present Levels of Performance: Another term for PLAAFP, describing a student's current abilities and challenges.

PT   Physical Therapy: A related service provided to students who need help improving motor skills or mobility.

PTI   Parent Training and Information Center: Federally funded center that provides support and resources to families of children with disabilities.

PWN   Prior Written Notice: A written document schools must provide when they propose or refuse changes to a child's education plan.

Response to Intervention (RTI)   A process used by educators to help students who are struggling with a skill or lesson. If a child does not respond to the initial interventions, more focused interventions are used to help the child master the skill. RTI strategies address both learning and behavior.

SDI   Specially Designed Instruction: Instruction tailored to meet the unique needs of a child with a disability.

SEA   State Education Agency: The state-level organization responsible for overseeing public education, including special education.

Section 504   A section of the Rehabilitation Act of 1973 that ensures students with disabilities have equal access to education through accommodations and modifications.

SLD   Specific Learning Disability: An IDEA category covering difficulties with reading, writing, or math that are not due to intellectual disabilities.

SLI   Speech or Language Impairment: An IDEA category for students with challenges in communication, such as articulation or expressive/receptive language.

SOP   Summary of Performance: A document provided to students with disabilities when they graduate or age out of special education services, summarizing their achievements and supports.

SPED   Special Education: A broad term for programs and services provided to students with disabilities.

TBI   Traumatic Brain Injury: An IDEA category for students with brain injuries that affect their ability to learn or function in school.

Transition Plan   A required section of the IEP for students age 16+ (or younger, depending on the state) to prepare for post-secondary goals in education, employment, and independent living.

TTD   Telecommunication Device for the Deaf: A device used to help individuals with hearing impairments communicate.

VI   Visual Impairment: An IDEA category covering partial or complete loss of vision that impacts education.

YTP   Youth Transition Program: Programs designed to support students with disabilities as they transition to adulthood.

Appendix B: IEP Meeting: Readiness Checklist

Let's be honest: IEP meetings can be overwhelming even for the most seasoned advocates. This checklist is here to help you feel more prepared and in control going into your next meeting.

Use this tool as a quick, practical way to check your readiness before the big day. It covers everything from reviewing your child's current IEP and progress data, to gathering your questions and concerns, to organizing any documentation you may want to bring.

This isn't about being perfect: It's about being prepared. When you walk into that meeting with a clear game plan, you're better positioned to speak up, ask the right questions, and make informed decisions for your child.

Whether you use this checklist a week before the meeting or the night before (we've all been there!), it's designed to ground you and reduce that last-minute scramble.

- ☐ Reviewed current IEP with notes and highlighter.
- ☐ Wrote a thorough list of parent concerns and emailed it.
- ☐ Completed a vision statement with family (Chapter 8).
- ☐ Talked with my child about attending the meeting, gave them opportunity to self-advocate.
- ☐ In agreement with other parent about issues, if applicable.
- ☐ If applicable, talked with Advocate about last-minute details.
- ☐ Compiled a list of my child's strengths and ideas how to leverage them.
- ☐ Reviewed necessary school district policies (attendance, discipline).
- ☐ Compiled a list of suggested goals or interventions that need to be changed.
- ☐ Rehearsed difficult conversations in my head or in front of mirror (or in car).
- ☐ Have printouts about child's condition from Internet or from specialists.
- ☐ Researched evaluations and strategies for child's issues.
- ☐ RSVP'd to meeting with expectations of who I expect to be there.
- ☐ Have childcare for other children or requested time off work.
- ☐ Have outfit picked out (for confidence).
- ☐ Cleared schedule day before and after meeting (for prep and rest or self-care afterward).

Appendix C: IEP Meeting: Notes Template

Trying to take notes during an IEP meeting while also staying present, asking questions, and advocating is a lot. That's why I created this simple notes template to help you stay organized and capture the most important pieces of the conversation without feeling scattered or overwhelmed.

This template gives you space to jot down what each team member says, track decisions that were made, and flag anything that needs follow-up. You can print it and bring it with you to the meeting or use it to type up your notes afterward while everything is still fresh.

Bonus tip: These notes are also a great way to create your post-meeting follow-up letter if needed. You'll already have everything documented in one place.

Use it your way: before, during, or after the meeting.

IEP Meeting Notes

Introductions, Review Last Year's IEP	Vision Statement from Family	
Evaluation Reports and Present Levels	IEP Goals and Progress Monitoring	Special Factors and Disability Category
Interventions, SDIs, Related Services	Transition Planning	

Appendix D: IEP Meeting: Questions to Ask

As a parent and as an effective parent advocate, you should have the answers to all these questions. No, I'm not suggesting that you ask 30 questions at your IEP meeting. But to be an effective advocate for your child, you should have the answers or know where to find the answers, to these questions.

Here are 30 questions you can ask at an IEP meeting to ensure your children's needs are being addressed and their educational goals are being met:

1. What is the process for determining my child's present levels of performance?
2. How is my chlidren's progress toward their IEP goals being measured?
3. Can you explain how my child's strengths and weaknesses are incorporated into the IEP?
4. What specific accommodations and modifications will my child receive in the classroom?
5. What type of support do my children need for their social and emotional development?
6. How will my child's sensory needs be addressed in the classroom?
7. What is the plan for my child's transition from one grade to the next?
8. How often will my child's progress be monitored and how will we receive updates?
9. What goals are being set for my child this year? Are these goals measurable and achievable?
10. Can you explain how my children's specific learning needs are addressed in their goals?
11. Who will be working with my child on these goals, and what are their qualifications?
12. How does the school ensure that my child is included in general education activities to the greatest extent possible?
13. What services are being provided outside of the classroom (e.g., speech therapy, OT, counseling)?
14. Is there a plan in place for addressing behavioral issues if they arise?
15. What strategies are being used to support my child's executive functioning skills?
16. How will technology be integrated into my child's learning if at all?
17. What is the school's plan for ensuring my child has a safe, supportive environment?
18. What are the criteria for determining if my child needs additional services or interventions?
19. How are the goals aligned with state standards or grade-level expectations?
20. What will be the communication plan between the school and our family?
21. Is there a process for requesting a change to the individualized educational program (IEP) if we feel it's not working?

22. How does the school ensure that the IEP is being implemented as written?
23. What steps are taken if my child struggles with the IEP goals?
24. How does the school handle bullying or other social issues affecting my child?
25. What is the plan for my child's future education or post-secondary transition goals?
26. How does the school ensure that my child has access to extracurricular activities?
27. Is there a backup plan if the interventions or supports provided are not working as expected?
28. What professional development is the staff receiving related to my child's disability?
29. How are my child's mental health needs addressed in the IEP?
30. Can you explain how parent input is incorporated into the development of the IEP?

These questions will help you better understand the process and ensure that your child's educational needs are being met effectively.

Appendix E: Parent-Teacher Conference: Questions to Ask

While parent-teacher conferences and individualized education program (IEP) meetings both focus on your child's education, they serve very different purposes, which shapes the questions you ask in each setting. A parent-teacher conference is generally a short, informal conversation about your child's overall performance in the classroom. It's a chance to get a snapshot of how your child is doing academically, socially, and behaviorally from the teacher's perspective. In contrast, an IEP meeting is a structured, legally required process to review, revise, and ensure the implementation of your child's IEP.

The primary difference lies in the scope and focus. Parent-teacher conferences are usually centered on general classroom performance and are often led by one teacher. They provide an opportunity to discuss grades, classroom behavior, and how your child interacts with peers. The discussion is typically broad, covering what's working and where there may be room for improvement.

An IEP meeting, however, is far more detailed and collaborative. It involves a team of professionals, including special education staff, therapists, administrators, and sometimes even outside experts. The goal is to analyze your child's unique needs, set specific goals, and create a plan to provide individualized support. Unlike a parent-teacher conference, the IEP meeting is guided by federal law, such as the Individuals with Disabilities Education Act (IDEA), making it a formal and data-driven process.

Because of these differences, the questions you ask at an IEP meeting should focus on measurable progress, data, and services that address your child's unique needs. In a parent-teacher conference, your questions might aim to gain insights into day-to-day classroom activities and how your child fits into the broader educational environment. At an IEP meeting, you're not just looking for a general update; instead, you're there to hold the team accountable for implementing the IEP and ensuring it's effective.

The stakes are also different. A parent-teacher conference might help you identify areas for improvement, but the decisions made in an IEP meeting directly impact the services, supports, and accommodations your child will receive. This makes IEP meetings critical for ensuring your child's educational success. Understanding the distinctions between these meetings will help you approach each one with the right mindset and prepare accordingly.

Questions to Ask at your Parent-Teacher Conference

1. How is their progress being tracked? Can I see the data?
2. What progress has my child made toward (a specific IEP goal or objective)?
3. Are there any goals that you are feeling are not appropriate, now that we are three months into the year?

4. Are there any strategies you would suggest adding to support them with the challenging goals?

5. Are my children's behavior or focus affecting their learning? How is that being addressed?

6. How are accommodations being used in the classroom?

7. Can you walk me through a typical day for my child?

8. Are there any concerns about their social interactions with peers? Do they have friends?

9. What should I be doing at home to support their progress?

10. Have there been any changes in their attitude toward school or learning?

11. Are my children receiving their related services as listed in the IEP, e.g., Occupational Therapy (OT), Physical Therapy (PT), speech? How is that going?

12. Are the accommodations listed in the IEP or 504 plan enough, or do you see areas where we need to make changes?

13. How is my child being supported during less structured times like lunch or recess?

14. Are there any extracurricular activities or programs that could benefit my child?

15. What's one thing my child does well that you wish you could see more of?

16. Do you feel my child is being challenged enough academically?

17. How are you managing my child's sensory needs (if applicable)?

18. Are there upcoming classroom changes (e.g., new units, projects) that might present challenges for my child?

19. Is the IEP or 504 plan being followed consistently by all teachers and staff?

20. What can we improve or adjust in the IEP or 504 to ensure my child continues making progress?

21. How are his or her grades and what do those grades measure? (Because remember, grades are subjective, not objective!)

22. Do you have any recent standardized test scores, e.g., Measures of Academic Progress (MAP)?

23. Do you have any behavior or incident reports?

24. Can you show me some examples of work (in area of concern)?

25. In the past 90 days, do you feel that the (academic, social, behavior) performance is getting better, worse, or staying the same?

26. Talk to your child beforehand, see if they have any questions they want you to ask.

27. Ask the teachers if they have any questions for you, about your child.

28. Do you feel this is the right placement for my child?

For more information, see **ADayInOurShoes.com**.

Appendix F: Goal, Specially Designed Instruction (SDI), and Progress Monitoring Example

This is best practice as far as having a measurable individualized education program (IEP) goal, the SDI or interventions listed, and the progress monitoring reports.

It certainly makes sense to have the goal, objectives (if applicable), SDI, and progress monitoring data all in one place. If your IEP team does not provide this in a format that is understandable, ask for a meeting to revise this.

See the example below.

V. GOALS AND OBJECTIVES (*Continued*)

MEASURABLE ANNUAL GOAL *Include: Condition, Name, Behavior, and Criteria (Refer to Annotated IEP for description of these components)*	Describe HOW the student's progress toward meeting this goal will be measured	Describe WHEN periodic reports on progress will be provided to parents
Gross Motor Kevin will demonstrate improved activity tolerance and fitness by increasing his average daily step count to 12,000. Baseline: Average daily step count 9,068.	Daily data collection	Quarterly

Report of Progress:

3rd Marking Period - 3 = Satisfactory Progress - Kevin is going on short walks several times a day. He goes outside to the courtyard and walks through the halls on a daily basis. Kevin also joins the group exercise for short periods of time.

Goal Specific SDI:

Kevin will be provided with a pedometer. He will have opportunities to use a therapy ball or trampoline or to participate in other movement activities. He will be encouraged to walk gradually longer distances during his daily schedule.

On the first page for this goal (above), you can see that the goal is measurable. It also lists the child's current baseline. We can see that the school will collect data daily on this goal, but the parent can expect the information quarterly. The goal-specific SDIs are also listed.

Then in the next image you can see the progress monitoring data that was shared with the parent.

The school also listed the reason for the decrease in progress in the second quarter. Because the cause (increased seizure activity) is not something a school nor a child can fix, no changes to the IEP are warranted. Had it been another reason, a change to this IEP may have been warranted.

V. GOALS AND OBJECTIVES (*Continued*)

Short-term objectives / Benchmarks	Level of Achievement	Method of Evaluation
Kevin will demonstrate improved activity tolerance and fitness by increasing his average daily step count to 9,500.	Average daily step count to 9,500.	Daily data collection through the use of a pedometer.

Report of Progress:

1st Marking Period - Adequate progress - Kevin has had a big improvement in consistency of walking this quarter. While he isn't walking longer distances each walk, he is willing to walk more often during the school day with significantly less flopping behaviors. He continues to have a wide stance but he is walking with improved hip and knee extension and consequently has a much improved upright posture. His overall gait is gradually looking less unsteady as he improves his ability to navigate objects in his way by either stepping over them or moving around them.

2nd Marking Period - 2 - Inconsistent performance - Kevin continues to be more comfortable walking with less encouragement needed and increased flexibility with route and distance. His average overall step count, however, has been limited by days with increased seizure activity. During this quarter, his average step count was 8,365. We will continue to provide frequent opportunities for Kevin to walk in order to further increase his independence and activity tolerance.

3rd Marking Period - 3 = Satisfactory Progress -

Kevin will demonstrate improved activity tolerance and fitness by increasing his average daily step count to 10,000.	Average daily step count to 10,000.	Daily data collection through the use of a pedometer

Report of Progress:

Kevin will demonstrate improved activity tolerance and fitness by increasing his average daily step count to 11,000.	Average daily step count to 11,000.	Daily data collection through the use of a pedometer.

Report of Progress:

Appendix G: IEP Evaluations Checklist

Evaluations are the foundation of your child's IEP; without good data, it's nearly impossible to create meaningful goals or determine the right supports. This checklist is here to help you stay on top of the evaluation process from start to finish.

Whether you're requesting an initial evaluation, a re-evaluation, or an Independent Educational Evaluation (IEE), this tool walks you through what areas you may want the team to assess. It's a way to make sure nothing slips through the cracks because let's face it, there's a lot to track.

IEP Areas of Evaluation Checklist

These are some of the common areas of need for a child receiving IEP evaluations. Use this list as a guide to request IEP evaluations, re-evaluations, your Parent Concerns Letter or to add to the Permission to Evaluate form you receive.

Notes

- Academic Information
- Achievement vs. Ability
- Classroom Performance
- Adaptive Skills
- Assistive Technology
- Behavior- FBA
- Communication
- Developmental Skills
- Executive Functioning Skills
- Health
- Hearing
- Intellectual Ability
- Fine Motor Skills
- Gross Motor Skills
- Observations
- Perceptual Motor
- Social Skills/SEL
- Transition Assessments
- Voc Readiness, Interest/Preference
- Functional Voc Skills Assessment
- Vision-FVA
- Math and Money Skills

Appendix H: IEP Goal Tracker

It's surprisingly common to come across individualized education programs (IEPs) where there's little to no progress over multiple years, yet the plan doesn't change much to reflect that. Another thing I've seen more than once is what I call the "disappearing goal." A goal will appear on the IEP for a while, and then, without explanation, it's just gone.

IEPs do not exist in isolation, and it is not just important to learn and use progress monitoring as discussed in Chapter 22; you must also compare your IEP to the previous year's IEP. I created the IEP Goal Tracking Graphic Organizer to make this process easier for parents.

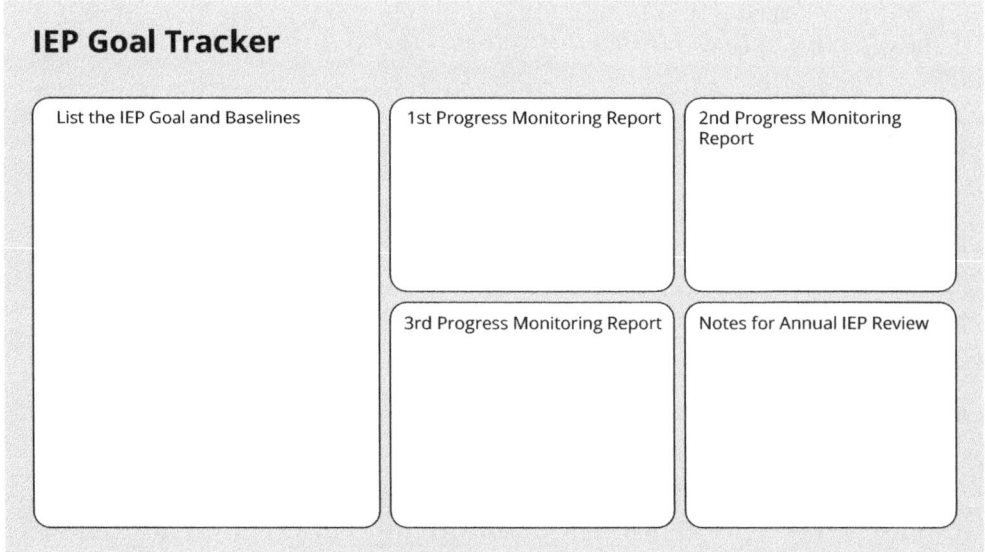

IEP Goal Tracker

List the IEP Goal and Baselines	1st Progress Monitoring Report	2nd Progress Monitoring Report
	3rd Progress Monitoring Report	Notes for Annual IEP Review

An IEP Goal Tracking Graphic Organizer is a powerful tool for parents to monitor their child's progress and ensure that the IEP goals are being addressed effectively.

Here's how you might use it:

Start with the IEP Goal and Baseline

- Write the Goal: Begin by transferring the IEP goal from the IEP document to the designated space on the graphic organizer. This ensures you always have a clear, accessible reference for what the goal is.

- Record the Baseline Data: Include the starting point (baseline) for that goal. For example, if the goal is for your child to read 30 words per minute and the baseline is 15 words per minute, write down the baseline for context.

Enter Progress Monitoring Data Regularly

- Use the spaces provided to document progress monitoring data from the reports the school sends home.
- For example, if progress reports are issued quarterly, record the data points (e.g., 20 words per minute in Q1, 25 words per minute in Q2).

Look for Trends

- As you fill in the data over time, use the organizer to spot patterns. Is progress steady? Are there periods of stagnation or regression?
- This visual representation makes it easier to see if the goal is on track to be met within the IEP period.

Identify and Document Concerns

- If the data show little to no progress, note your concerns directly on the organizer. For example:

    "Progress has stalled since Q2. Goal unlikely to be met without additional supports."
- This documentation can be helpful when advocating for changes in services or supports.

Prepare for IEP Meetings

- Bring the completed organizer to IEP meetings. Use it to demonstrate progress (or lack thereof) with concrete, organized data.
- This can support requests for adjustments, such as additional services, changes to accommodations, or new goals.

Make Informed Decisions

- The organizer allows you to track whether the interventions and supports in place are effective.
- Use the information to advocate for changes if the data suggests that your child isn't making meaningful progress.

By regularly using this IEP Goal Tracking Graphic Organizer, you can stay organized, spot issues early, and prevent a big problem from being a gigantic problem. Do not wait until a child is not making progress or regressing for an entire year before you address it. This graphic organizer also ensures that goals don't just mysteriously disappear.

This tool makes monitoring less overwhelming and helps turn a sea of data into actionable insights. A PDF copy for printing is available at **adayinourshoes.com/playbook**.

Appendix I: "The List"

Earlier in the book, I told you that there is no "list" and that when it comes to asking for goals, supports or placement for your child, there is no list provided to you by schools for what they can offer. I lied, sort of.

I maintain many such lists on my site **ADayInOurShoes.com**. I still would not expect your IEP team to provide you with such a list, but that doesn't mean you can't use the Internet to help you come up with ideas to bring to the table.

This appendix offers "the list" of the most popular topics from my site (**uadayinour shoes.com**).

I want to remind everyone that you cannot teach a set of skills if the child does not have the foundational knowledge or if all the proper assessments have not been done. For example, a child who does not get help with pragmatic language skills will continue to struggle with social skills. Students should not be given a checklist to help with executive functioning deficits causing forgotten homework; they'll just forget the checklist, too. Most of the time, our kids' issues and skill deficits do not exist in isolation.

Placement Options

I cannot provide a list of every private special needs school in the country. But I can share with you the continuum of Least Restrictive Environment (LRE). Remember, your team is required to consider LRE, but that does not mean that your child has to try every placement option.

Here is a list of eight options on this continuum, starting with the least restrictive:

1. **General Education Classroom with No Additional Supports**
   - Your child remains fully integrated with peers in a general education classroom without requiring additional accommodations or services.

2. **General Education Classroom with Support**
   - Accommodations or modifications are provided, e.g., preferential seating, assistive technology (AT), or differentiated instruction.
   - Related services such as speech therapy or Occupational Therapy (OT) might be delivered within the general classroom.

3. **General Education Classroom with Pull-Out Services**
   - Your child participates in General Education (GEN ED) for most of the day but is pulled out for specific services like resource room instruction or therapy.

4. **Resource Room**
   - A dedicated space where students receive specialized instruction in certain subjects or skills for part of the day while spending the rest of their time in the GEN ED classroom.

5. **Special Education Classroom**
   - A self-contained classroom where students with disabilities receive instruction tailored to their individual needs. Integration with non-disabled peers occurs during lunch, recess, or specials.

6. **Specialized Schools**
   - Students attend schools specifically designed for those with disabilities, offering tailored programs and expertise not available in traditional schools.

7. **Homebound or Hospital Instruction**
   - For students with medical or emotional needs that prevent regular school attendance. Education is delivered at home or in a medical setting.

8. **Residential Programs**
   - For students requiring intensive, round-the-clock services that cannot be met in a day school setting.

The goal of the Least Restrictive Environment (LRE) continuum is to provide an appropriate education in the setting that allows for the greatest possible interaction with non-disabled peers while meeting the student's educational needs. LRE means the least restrictive option for that child. It does not mean everyone has to be in a general education setting.

Executive Functioning

Executive functioning skills is the skill set I get the most questions about. Executive functions are a set of mental skills that include working memory, flexible thinking, and self-control, enabling individuals to plan, focus attention, manage tasks, and regulate behavior. They are essential for goal-directed activities and problem solving in daily life. If you want more information on executive functioning, I recommend Tera Sumpter and Seeds of Learning.

10 IEP Goal Ideas for Executive Functioning

Executive functioning challenges can show up in all kinds of ways, like difficulty starting tasks, managing time, staying organized, or remembering multi-step directions. These struggles can seriously impact a student's ability to succeed in school, but they're often overlooked when writing IEP goals.

This list includes 10 sample IEP goal ideas that target common executive functioning skills. These aren't copy-and-paste goals; instead, they're meant to spark ideas and help you advocate for supports that are tailored to your child's needs. Each goal focuses on building practical, measurable skills that can make day-to-day school life a little more manageable.

Whether you're drafting new goals or looking to revise existing ones, this list is a great place to start.

1. Time Management: The student will use a visual or digital timer to allocate appropriate time to complete tasks in 80% of opportunities as measured by teacher observation.

2. Organization: The student will independently maintain an organized workspace or desk and turn in assignments on time in four out of five observed instances.

3. Task Initiation: The student will independently begin tasks or activities within two minutes of being given instructions in 80% of opportunities.

4. Task Completion: The student will break down a multi-step assignment into smaller tasks and complete them in the assigned order in three out of four assignments.

5. Self-Regulation: The student will identify and use a calming strategy (e.g., deep breathing, taking a break) during moments of frustration in four out of five instances.

6. Working Memory: The student will follow multi-step oral directions (e.g., "Get your book, turn to page 15, and start reading") with 80% accuracy as measured by teacher data.

7. Prioritization: The student will create a prioritized to-do list for assignments or tasks and follow it with 90% accuracy during weekly planner checks.

8. Problem-Solving: The student will use a structured problem-solving strategy (e.g., identify the problem, brainstorm solutions, choose and try one) to resolve academic or peer-related challenges in four out of five observed instances.

9. Impulse Control: The student will pause and think before responding in class discussions or social interactions in eight out of ten opportunities as measured by teacher observation.

10. Planning: The student will use a graphic organizer to plan and organize ideas for a writing task in three out of four assignments.

20 Accommodation Ideas for Executive Functioning

Students with executive functioning challenges often need more than just goals; they need the right supports built into their school day. That's where accommodations come in.

This list includes 20 practical accommodation ideas that can help address common executive functioning struggles like organization, time management, task initiation, and working memory. These suggestions are designed to support students across different settings, whether they're in general education, special education, or a combination of both.

Use this list as a starting point when preparing for your next IEP meeting or 504 Plan discussion. The right accommodations can reduce stress and help your children access learning in a way that works for them.

Planning and Organization

1. Provide a daily or weekly planner with teacher support to track assignments and deadlines.
2. Break assignments into smaller, manageable steps with clear deadlines for each step.
3. Offer visual schedules or task charts to outline daily routines and activities.
4. Provide templates or graphic organizers for written work or projects.
5. Use color-coded folders or binders to organize materials for each subject.

Task Initiation and Completion

6. Offer frequent reminders or prompts to begin tasks, such as verbal cues or sticky notes.
7. Allow extra time to start and complete tasks, especially multi-step assignments.
8. Provide a checklist for students to mark off completed steps during tasks.
9. Pair verbal instructions with written ones to support task comprehension and initiation.
10. Assign a peer buddy for guidance in starting or organizing assignments.

Time Management

11. Use visual timers or digital reminders to help students manage time during activities.
12. Break long tasks into shorter work periods with scheduled breaks in between.
13. Allow flexible deadlines when appropriate, especially for larger projects.
14. Teach and model time estimation strategies for homework or classwork.

Memory and Attention

15. Provide a written summary of key points from lessons or class discussions.
16. Use apps or tools for reminders, such as calendar alerts or task management software.
17. Repeat or rephrase instructions as needed to support working memory.
18. Encourage the use of sticky notes for jotting down reminders or instructions.

Self-Regulation

19. Offer access to a quiet space or sensory area for breaks when feeling overwhelmed.
20. Teach and support the use of self-monitoring tools, such as reflection journals or behavior tracking sheets.

Social Skills or Social Emotional Learning

Social skills and social-emotional learning (SEL) involve understanding and managing emotions, building healthy relationships, and making responsible decisions. These skills enable individuals to navigate social situations effectively, empathize with others, and communicate appropriately.

Social skills are an essential part of school success, but they don't always come naturally for every student. Whether it's making friends, joining group activities, understanding social cues, or managing emotions in conversations, these skills can be taught and supported through well-written IEP goals.

This list includes 10 sample IEP goal ideas focus on different areas of social development. They're designed to give you a starting point when advocating for your child's needs, especially if social skills challenges are impacting their school experience.

10 IEP Goals for Social Skills

1. Initiating Conversations: The student will independently initiate a conversation with a peer or adult using a greeting and a question in four out of five opportunities as measured by teacher observation.

2. Maintaining Conversations: The student will maintain a conversation by responding appropriately to questions or comments and asking a follow-up question in three out of five observed instances.

3. Recognizing Social Cues: The student will identify and interpret basic social cues (e.g., facial expressions, tone of voice) in four out of five scenarios as measured by teacher-created assessments.

4. Sharing and Turn-Taking: The student will take turns during group activities or games without prompts in 80% of opportunities.

5. Conflict Resolution: The student will use a taught conflict resolution strategy (e.g., I-messages, taking turns speaking) to resolve disagreements with peers in four out of five observed instances.

6. Listening and Clarifying: Students will ask for clarification (e.g., "Can you repeat that?") when they do not understand a verbal instruction in three out of five instances.

7. Basic Group Engagement: The student will participate in group activities by contributing one idea or answer in four out of five opportunities.

8. Collaboration on Projects: The student will contribute to a group project by completing assigned tasks and sharing results in three out of four group activities.

9. Empathy Skills: The student will identify how others might feel in a given scenario and suggest a supportive response in three out of four trials.

10. Problem Solving in Social Situations: The student will identify a social problem and brainstorm at least two potential solutions in four out of five scenarios.

20 Accommodations or Teaching Strategies for Social Skills

Supporting social skill development takes more than just setting a goal. It often requires intentional accommodations and teaching strategies built into the school day.

This list offers 20 ideas that can help students who struggle with things like peer interactions, reading social cues, managing emotions, or participating in group work. Some items are accommodations that can be written into an IEP or 504 Plan, while others are strategies teachers and staff can use during instruction and unstructured times.

Direct Instruction and Modeling

1. Teach social skills explicitly using role-playing scenarios.

2. Model appropriate social interactions and provide opportunities for the student to practice with feedback.

3. Use social stories to explain expected behaviors in specific situations.

4. Implement video modeling by showing examples of positive social interactions.

5. Provide direct instruction on recognizing and interpreting facial expressions and body language.

Environmental Supports

6. Assign a peer buddy or mentor to support social engagement during group activities.

7. Create structured opportunities for social interaction, such as small group work or cooperative learning activities.

8. Arrange seating to encourage interaction with peers who model positive social behaviors.

9. Provide a quiet or sensory-friendly space for students to decompress when overwhelmed by social situations.

10. Use visual supports, such as cue cards or posters, to remind students of social expectations.

Feedback and Reinforcement

11. Provide immediate, specific feedback on social interactions to reinforce appropriate behaviors.

12. Use positive reinforcement, such as a token system or praise, to encourage social engagement.

13. Set up a reward system for meeting specific social goals (e.g., using a calm voice during disagreements).

Practice Opportunities

14. Schedule structured practice sessions to rehearse social skills, such as role-playing, greeting someone, or resolving conflicts.

15. Include the student in extracurricular activities or clubs that align with their interests to practice social skills in a natural setting.

16. Encourage participation in group games or sports to practice teamwork and communication.

Communication Supports

17. Teach the use of scripts or sentence starters for common social situations (e.g., "Can I play with you?" or "Thank you for helping me").

18. Provide access to a communication device or alternative communication methods if verbal communication is challenging.

19. Use visual cues (e.g., pictures or gestures) to prompt appropriate social responses.

Collaborative Supports

20. Collaborate with a speech therapist or social worker to incorporate social skills training into therapy sessions or group activities.

Reading and Writing

What's happening today in schools with so many kids struggling to read and write and not being given the appropriate interventions should be criminal. This is one learning disability where I witness parents being dismissed and gaslit the most. "He's fine!" and similar sentiments when the child is not fine.

It takes a lot of persistence, but keep at it. The Decoding Dyslexia groups are great for specific information and I think every state has a chapter. The movies/documentary "The Right to Read" and "Left Behind" are excellent.

10 IEP Goals for Reading

Here's a list of 10 IEP goal ideas and 20 accommodations/teaching strategies for reading and writing, tailored to address different needs and skill levels:

1. Reading Fluency: The student will read a grade-level passage aloud at a rate of 100 words per minute with 95% accuracy in four out of five trials.
2. Phonics: The student will decode consonant-vowel-consonant (CVC) words with 90% accuracy in four out of five opportunities.
3. Sight Words: The student will recognize and read 50 high-frequency sight words from a targeted list with 90% accuracy.
4. Comprehension—Main Idea: The student will identify the main idea of a grade-level paragraph in four out of five attempts.
5. Inferencing: The student will use context clues to infer the meaning of unknown words in a text with 80% accuracy.
6. Sequencing: The student will retell key events from a story in the correct sequence in four out of five opportunities.
7. Vocabulary: The student will learn and use 10 new vocabulary words related to classroom content each week, demonstrating understanding through sentences or definitions.
8. Reading Comprehension—Details: Students will answer four out of five questions about key details in a passage at their instructional level.
9. Making Predictions: The student will make logical predictions about a text based on the title, illustrations, and first paragraph in four out of five trials.
10. Compare and Contrast: The student will compare and contrast two characters, events, or settings from a story using a graphic organizer in three out of four assignments.

10 IEP Goals for Writing

Writing is one of the most complex academic skills because it pulls together organization, fine motor skills, spelling, grammar, and more. This list of IEP goal ideas covers a range of writing challenges, from forming complete sentences to planning multi-paragraph essays. Use these examples to help guide conversations with your IEP team and develop goals that meet your child's individual needs.

1. Sentence Writing: The student will write complete sentences with correct capitalization and punctuation in four out of five attempts.
2. Paragraph Writing: The student will write a structured paragraph with a topic sentence, supporting details, and a conclusion in three out of four trials.
3. Grammar: The student will correctly use common punctuation marks (periods, commas, question marks) in their writing with 80% accuracy.
4. Spelling: The student will spell grade-level words correctly in four out of five written assignments.
5. Handwriting: The student will write legibly, using appropriate letter size, spacing, and alignment in 80% of written work.
6. Organization: The student will use a graphic organizer to plan a writing task in three out of four assignments.
7. Editing and Revising: Students will independently revise and edit their writing to improve grammar, spelling, and structure in three out of five assignments.
8. Opinion Writing: The student will write an opinion piece that includes a clear opinion, supporting reasons, and a conclusion in four out of five opportunities.
9. Creative Writing: The student will write a short story with a clear beginning, middle, and end in three out of four attempts.
10. Research Skills: The student will write a short research-based paragraph using at least two sources, including a citation, in three out of four trials.

20 Accommodations or Teaching Strategies for Reading and Writing

Reading and writing challenges can show up in so many different ways, and often, kids need more than just goals. This list includes practical accommodations and teaching strategies to support students with decoding, comprehension, written expression, spelling, and more.

Whether you're looking to support a struggling reader, a reluctant writer, or a student with dyslexia or a language-based learning disability, these ideas can help create a more accessible and supportive learning environment.

Use this list as a tool during IEP meetings or when brainstorming with your children's team about what might help them succeed.

For Reading

1. Provide access to audiobooks or text-to-speech software.
2. Highlight key information in reading materials to improve focus on essential details.
3. Use graphic organizers (e.g., story maps, cause-and-effect charts) to aid comprehension.
4. Break reading assignments into shorter, manageable sections.
5. Provide a preview of vocabulary before reading a text.
6. Allow extra time for reading assignments and assessments.
7. Pair texts with visuals or videos to enhance understanding.
8. Use guided reading groups to provide targeted instruction at the student's reading level.
9. Provide frequent check-ins to monitor comprehension during independent reading.
10. Teach phonics and decoding skills explicitly using a multisensory approach, e.g., Orton-Gillingham (OG).

For Writing

11. Allow the use of typing or speech-to-text software for written assignments.
12. Provide a word bank or sentence starters to support sentence construction.
13. Offer extended time for writing tasks and projects.
14. Use graphic organizers to plan essays, stories, or reports.
15. Teach spelling patterns and rules explicitly using a structured program.
16. Provide rubrics or checklists to guide the writing process.
17. Allow oral responses instead of written work for some assignments.
18. Pair the student with a peer editor to review drafts together.
19. Provide frequent feedback during the writing process rather than just at the end.
20. Use scaffolded templates for structured writing tasks (e.g., fill-in-the-blank outlines for paragraphs).

Behavior Goals and Accommodations

I have a lot of information on my site about behavior. And this is an area where my philosophy and opinion have changed due to learning from families I serve.

I'm in the camp that if your children have the right IEP for them and it's being implemented with fidelity, there won't be negative behaviors resulting from unmet needs. If you get the chance, look up Ross Greene. His statement of "Kids do well when they can" is something I repeat often.

"All behavior tells you something" but in my professional experience, the adults around the child with the behaviors aren't digging deep enough to figure out what the something is.

Still, your IEP team may want to do a Functional Behavior Assessment (FBA) and behavior plan, so it's best to have ideas. You can do both, meaning go along with the behavior plan but still dig into your IEP and see what might be changed to eliminate the behaviors.

10 IEP Goals for Behavior

Here are 10 IEP goal ideas and 20 accommodations/teaching strategies for behavior, focusing on areas like self-regulation, emotional control, and appropriate classroom conduct:

1. Self-Regulation: Students will identify their emotions using a visual chart and select an appropriate coping strategy in four out of five observed instances.
2. Impulse Control: The student will follow classroom rules and refrain from interrupting during group discussions in 80% of opportunities as measured by teacher observation.
3. Transition Management: The student will transition between activities within the classroom without displaying disruptive behaviors in four out of five opportunities.
4. Anger Management: The student will use a taught calming strategy (e.g., deep breathing, counting to 10) to manage frustration before it escalates in four out of five situations.
5. On-Task Behavior: The student will remain focused on a given task for 15 minutes with no more than one prompt in four out of five opportunities.
6. Conflict Resolution: The student will resolve conflicts with peers using a taught strategy (e.g., "I feel" statements) in four out of five observed instances.
7. Respectful Communication: The student will use appropriate language and tone when addressing teachers and peers in four out of five opportunities.
8. Following Directions: The student will follow multi-step directions without additional prompts in 80% of trials.
9. Replacement Behaviors: The student will use a replacement behavior (e.g., raising a hand instead of shouting out) in 80% of opportunities as measured by teacher data.
10. Social Skills: The student will engage in positive peer interactions during unstructured activities (e.g., recess) in three out of four observed instances.

20 Accommodations or Teaching Strategies for Behavior

Environmental Supports

1. Create a structured classroom routine with clear expectations displayed visually.
2. Use a visual schedule to help the student anticipate transitions and changes in activities.
3. Provide access to a quiet, calming area for self-regulation when the student feels overwhelmed.

4. Use proximity control by seating the student near the teacher or positive peer role models.

5. Minimize distractions by providing a structured workspace with limited visual and auditory stimuli.

Behavior Supports

6. Develop a Behavior Intervention Plan (BIP) that includes specific strategies for managing challenging behaviors.

7. Provide frequent positive reinforcement (e.g., praise, tokens, or tangible rewards) for appropriate behavior.

8. Use a check-in/check-out system with a trusted staff member to support daily behavior goals.

9. Implement a token economy system to reward positive behaviors and reinforce desired actions.

10. Provide clear, consistent consequences for positive and negative behaviors.

Self-Regulation Strategies

11. Teach and model calming techniques, such as deep breathing, mindfulness exercises, or progressive muscle relaxation.

12. Provide access to sensory tools (e.g., stress balls, fidgets, weighted blankets) to help the student regulate emotions.

13. Allow breaks during tasks or activities to reduce frustration or overstimulation.

14. Use social stories to teach appropriate responses to specific situations (e.g., handling anger or disappointment).

Instructional Supports

15. Provide step-by-step instructions with visual aids to help the student follow directions.

16. Use verbal and non-verbal cues (e.g., a hand signal or a tap on the desk) to redirect the student discreetly.

17. Allow for movement breaks to help the student release excess energy and refocus.

18. Provide structured opportunities for practicing replacement behaviors in controlled settings.

19. Use small group or individual instruction to teach and reinforce social-emotional learning (SEL) skills.

Collaboration and Monitoring

20. Collaborate with parents and related service providers (e.g., counselors, occupational therapists) to ensure consistency in behavior strategies across settings.

About the Author

Lisa Lightner is a nationally recognized special education advocate, parent, and the creator of *A Day in Our Shoes*, an online resource for families navigating the IEP process. Since 2010, Lisa has supported thousands of parents through one-on-one advocacy, empowering them to understand their rights, communicate effectively with school teams, and ensure meaningful progress for their children.

Lisa has served on the boards of several disability-related nonprofits and advocacy organizations, listening to the disability community and broadening her perspective on systemic change as an active lobbyist.

In addition to *A Day in our Shoes*, Lisa started *Don't IEP Alone* in 2020, which is online tools and training for both parents and school staff. Her work has been featured in national media, parent training, and school districts across the country. She is a fierce believer in informed advocacy and never attends an IEP meeting without a plan. There's also plenty of information on my sites (**adayinourshoes.com** and **dontiepalone.com**).

Acknowledgments

I have been fortunate to work alongside an incredible community of families, advocates, and professionals who made this book possible.

First, I want to acknowledge my family. To my sons, Kevin and Brian: Kevin, who gave me the lived experience that started this journey, and Brian, who continues to fuel my motivation. You both mean more to me than words can express. To my husband, Dan: thank you for your patience and unwavering support. You make it all possible.

To the thousands of parents in my online community who have reached out over the years through emails, comments, and speaking to your support groups. Thank you for trusting me with your stories, your frustrations, your questions, your IEP meetings, and your wins. This book exists because of you. Your feedback, encouragement, and tough questions pushed me to dig deeper and explain things better. You helped shape this work in ways you may not even realize.

I am grateful for the advocates, attorneys, educators, "policy wonks," and professionals who have shared their time, knowledge, and perspectives with me along the way. Special thanks to those who challenged me; that's where true growth happens.

I am especially thankful for the individuals who shaped the advocate I am today. While I fear leaving someone out, I want to recognize Christine, Angie, Blake, Jenny, Michelle, Gina, Cheryl-Lynn, Sabra, Saafir, Carolyn, Susan, Sherry, Bridget, and Laura for your influence, encouragement, and support.

And finally, to every child who sits through IEP meetings without ever being in the room, this is for you. You deserve an educational system that sees your strengths, supports your needs, and includes your voice. Always.

Printed and bound by CPI Group (UK) Ltd, Croydon, CR0 4YY

27/08/2025

14725038-0001

Printed and bound by CPI Group (UK) Ltd, Croydon, CR0 4YY

27/08/2025

14725038-0001